FINI

IN DEATH AND LIFE

A PASSAGE THROUGH GRIEF

LYNNE LITTLE

FINDING GOD IN DEATH AND LIFE

lynne@lynnelittle.org

Printed in the United States of America
First Printing, 2020
ISBN: 978-1-7353017-0-9

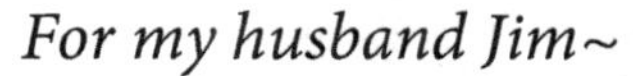

For my husband Jim~

The love of my life, and the kindest person I know.

TABLE OF CONTENTS

FOREWORD

On March 13, 2001, my only child, Lisa Joy, was killed in an automobile accident. In my first book, *Missing Lisa: A Parent Grieves*, I documented the details of the event, the terrible grief, and the crises of faith that resulted from the death of my beautiful daughter.

This book is a continuation of that journey. It is a collection of brief reflections on various topics pertaining to grief. These essays elaborate on an episode in my life that has to this day left me utterly changed. Some of the entries illuminate my thought processes as I worked through the many personal, doctrinal, and theological issues that arose as challenges to my faith. Others highlight the strategies I found to be most helpful in moving forward and wrestling purpose out of heartache.

Although the points of view that I present may perhaps seem atypical—disconcerting to some or unusual to others—I hope that the result will be a welcome measure of increased insight into realities that are anything but simple. Those whose hearts have been broken require stronger remedies than pat answers can provide.

As you grapple with grief and search for meaning in your loss, I hope that you will find comfort within these pages and discover the courage and resilience necessary to keep going.

Above all, may you draw strength and find peace and rest in the everlasting arms of the God who loves you unreservedly.

CHAPTER 1

FINDING GOD: MY STORY

My spiritual journey began with one simple prayer. At seven years of age, kneeling beside my grandmother at the foot of her little bed, I recited with her the "Sinner's Prayer."[1] I am not sure I fully understood everything the prayer meant, but I recall with remarkable clarity the warm and deeply reassuring sensations that accompanied it. With little reinforcement from my family—churchgoers who were nevertheless unaware of the process of achieving "salvation" as it was explained to me by my grandmother—and the unfortunate loss through the early death of my grandmother, who was my treasured spiritual mentor, my newfound faith, not surprisingly, floundered.

Occasionally, a flash of recognition or an insight of sorts, reminiscent of that first nascent faith, would come to me unannounced—such as when on a road trip our family stopped at a miniature golf course structured as a village scene complete with tiny chapel. As I stood behind the child-sized pulpit pretending to "preachify," there came an impression of almost inexpressible longing for something—or "Someone"—beyond myself. Such feelings came to me at seemingly random

[1] A fuller explanation of this prayer is presented in Chapter 4.

(yet, in retrospect, not so random) moments throughout my young life, during times of joy, or what passed for joy, such as when unwrapping presents on Christmas morning, and poignant sorrow, for instance when being ridiculed by siblings or classmates for being too *something*—sensitive or skinny or touchy or emotional or smarty pants—those slights and slurs that somehow unerringly target the very things you most often wish you could change about yourself.

It was during those times that an inexorable sense that I was not alone would wash over me, an understanding of sorts, that a Presence was near—indistinct but real—though not quite within my reach. This knowing was simultaneously accompanied by a longing for something different, or more, or better, or higher. What I actually wanted, I knew not, nor could I properly articulate. Later, I would recognize those feelings in the description of a sensation that Christian apologist C. S. Lewis once referred to as "that old ache." As a child, however, I had no substantive frame of reference for spiritual things and eventually convinced my young self to chalk these experiences up to emotional flights of fancy.

Fast forward to my middle school and early high school years when, dogged by the relentless self-doubts, insecurities, and heartaches of adolescence, I once again resumed the search for spiritual meaning. I read selections from the "isms" of major religions, credos, and political systems that nations and entire populations adhere to and espouse. I examined excerpts from the Bible, the Koran, and the Book of Mormon. I discussed with like-minded friends the philosophies of Plato, Socrates, Aristotle, Locke, Nietzsche and Kant and others until our heads positively ached from tracing their convoluted analytical switchbacks.

This collective "Tao" of viewpoints that I listened to and absorbed contained gems of valuable universal ethics or truths. Yet, they seemed to collectively decline to enunciate in plain speech that their way was unequivocally *the* way. Was philosophy the way? Was religion? I consulted Father Gus, a kindly "born again" Catholic priest who listened patiently as I peppered him with questions on the Bible, the teachings of the church, and the human condition.

Wrestling with weighty subjects such as creation, the meaning of life and the existence of evil, I examined the litany of solutions each "-ism" or point of view had to offer, trying on and summarily discarding one after the other while growing more exasperated in the process. Despairing of ever finding what I was looking for, I questioned the validity of my search for this diaphanous "Other-in-the-ether" and even the necessity of it, reasoning that most people my age were occupied with purely terrestrial concerns.

In the course of my search, I decided to eliminate from consideration all credos, philosophies, and systems that had no concept of a god at their center. Indeed, my recollected experiences most decidedly involved an interaction with a Being. I could not equate a strictly mental construct with the definitively palpable encounters of my past. I delved more completely into the study of systems of beliefs found in world religions. Eventually, amid the cacophony of incompatible claims, strikingly similar patterns emerged.

Although proponents made the same assertions that their way contained truth or a path to finding the truth, the systems they espoused were vastly different in tone and approach, which then raised the issue of whether truth was relative or changeable. Notwithstanding, there was one basic tenet many held in common and it was this: nearly every religion required onerous effort in the form of formulaic rituals, repetitive prayers, and sacrificial offerings by the individual to connect with a deity or deities who were exacting, intractable, quixotic, and in the end often totally unreachable. Somehow those "ways" were too contrived. Those "truths" did not, for me, ring true.

Compounding the situation, in most cases, adherents to these beliefs were provided no guarantee of a satisfactory outcome for a life well lived. In short, nothing conclusive regarding life after death was promised unless one considered martyrdom as the only effort worthy of reward. This dichotomy was deeply puzzling to me. I could not understand why the god or gods who may have perhaps been responsible for creating everything from the gorgeous, breathtakingly infinite universe to the single—once absurdly regarded as *simple*—cell within us, and therefore vastly superior to the human race in every way, would think it fair to require humans, who by comparison were fragile and minute, to somehow work their way arduously to a nexus with them.

This carrot-on-a-stick approach seemed to be the ultimate taunt—a deity dangling a tantalizing yet unreachable destiny—a cruel and sick cosmic joke played on gullible mankind. Who would want a deity so lacking in love and compassion? How could such a one evoke, indeed deserve, a disciple's loyalty and devotion? I wanted no part of a god who was not at least as kind, just, or approachable as my own father, of that I was certain. Thus, despite my search, I eventually reached a frustrating and seemingly insoluble impasse.

At this juncture, an idea occurred to me that seemed novel at the time, yet which I later found to be a common refrain among seekers of truth. I reasoned that if indeed there was a god who existed and who additionally wanted to be found and communicated with, it seemed logical to place on that being the responsibility for making the first move! In actuality, the prayer I recall praying, "*If you are real, please contact me*," was in essence *my* making the first move. The answer to this "leap of faith" was not long in coming, but it took a form I least expected.

A classmate invited me to a meeting held in her home that was sponsored by an organization known as Young Life. It was an evening of camaraderie, music, laughter, and interesting conversation—a buzz of joyful optimism unlike anything I had ever experienced. When the leader stood up to speak, I was transfixed. His talk began with a description of a deity who loved us unconditionally despite what He saw and understood of our flaws and foibles. He claimed that this God—who acknowledged the vast chasm that separated the creation from the Creator—had already prepared a unique provision to span the gap. The account of God's death to satisfy the claims of justice and atone for the sins of the world by acting as its scapegoat was somehow plausible to me in its sheer implausibility, for how could any human have invented such a brilliantly equitable solution?

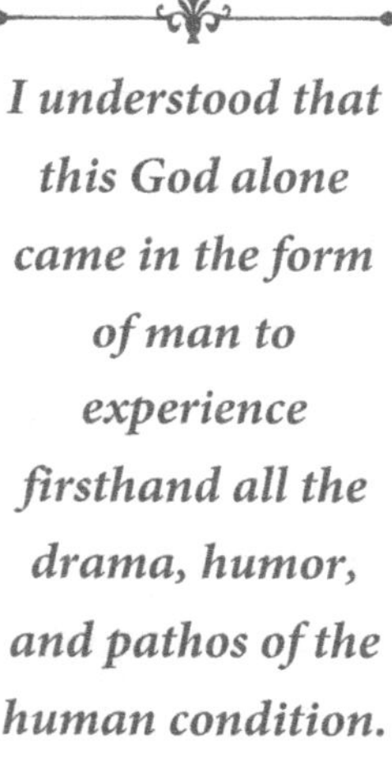

When the speaker stated, "…and Christ came down," a final piece of what had puzzled me for years clicked into place, for the one crucial element found wanting in all the gods of all the religions I had studied was the willingness of any god to meet mankind right where we were. I understood that this God alone came in the form of man to experience firsthand all the drama, humor, and pathos of the human condition. I heard that this God alone had granted mankind total access and offered a steadfast assurance to never leave or forsake any of his own. This God alone conferred a warranted future with the promise of assistance in the here and now. This God alone pledged all of Himself to woo mankind into a relationship with Him, an incredibly generous concession it seemed to me, coming from such a vastly omnipotent entity. This God personified the very definition of love. Who else loved that much and in quite that way?

Yet apparently, this God, and only this God, hinged eternity on a single condition, one of astounding import yet flawless simplicity, a condition so effortlessly met it seemed (to an incredulous me) almost too ridiculously easy. The condition was a prayer acknowledging the belief that Jesus Christ was the Son of God who died on the cross to deliver a new way of living to those who received Him. That prayer had a ring of familiarity. Hearing of it took me back to my innocent seven-year-old self and the extraordinary moment when I had, in simple faith, made that profession. Recognizing this, I reasoned that now might be an appropriate time to renew an old acquaintance.

Along with a roomful of people, I bowed my head, prayed that prayer, and in so doing, came face to face with Jesus, the One who had been there all along.

CHAPTER 2

LOOKING FOR GOD: PRACTICAL THEOLOGY

REVISITING A "BETRAYAL"

Faithful are the wounds of a friend, But the kisses of an enemy are deceitful.

—**Proverbs 27:6**

After saying these things, Jesus was troubled in his spirit, and testified, "Truly, truly, I say to you, one of you will betray me."

— **John 13:21**

My relationship with God was not the result of a *conversion* per se. I did not embrace Christianity based upon an intellectual assent to the doctrines of a religion. I don't even remember believing that my works or efforts could in any manner lead me to reconciliation with God.

My decision was instead based on the desire to know God in a personal way. When I made the decision to receive Christ, God began in me a life-changing, utterly transformative experience that continues to this day. I knew at the time that I was making a-no-holds-barred choice, one that once made would not be reversed. Indeed, I never wished for or even once entertained the idea of turning back.

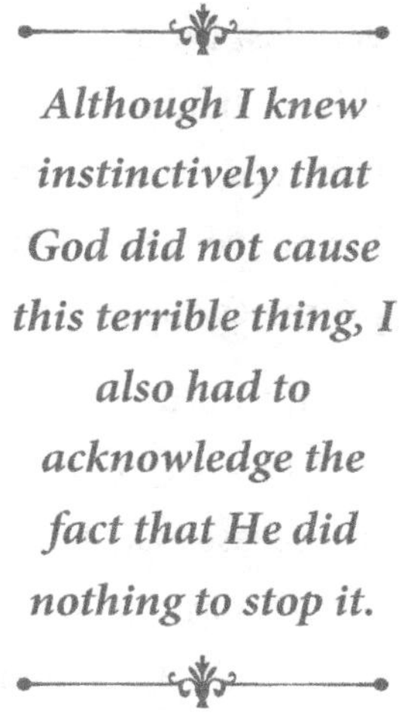

That is until my daughter died. Prior to that event, I had been experiencing a personal relationship with a God in whom I trusted completely. I never viewed my commitment as shallow or fragile. Yet during those first terrible days, the emotion I remember experiencing most keenly was a gut-wrenching feeling of total betrayal. Although I knew instinctively that God did not cause this terrible thing, I also had to acknowledge the fact that He did nothing to stop it.

Where do you turn when the very life you've lived and the Hope that has consistently been your north star, your guiding light—your *friend*—seems to have betrayed your trust? The very last thing I thought I would ever be confronted with was this particular crisis of faith. What was I supposed to do when betrayed by someone I deeply loved and trusted? How would I resolve the dissonance between promises made and promises apparently broken?

By all appearances, it looked as if the entire lot of a lifetime of Christian service—*years* spent in prayer, intercessions, teaching, mentoring, making disciples—would have to be scrapped *if* it had all been done in the Name of One who could no longer be trusted. My confusion deepened when I considered that Jesus had himself been the subject of a terrible betrayal.

In pondering this seemingly unsolvable dilemma, I recalled a story found in scripture that seemed to illustrate my conflict. The sixteenth chapter of Matthew describes two interesting scenarios that occurred back-to-back. In the first account, the disciple Peter received the revelation that Jesus is the Son of God. Jesus commended him for this. Yet, when shortly after this Jesus began to prepare His followers for His imminent death, Peter reacted in horror. According to Matthew 16:22, "Then Peter took Him (Jesus) aside and began to rebuke Him, saying, "Far be it from You, Lord; this shall not be unto You!" Peter's words indicated a deeply felt sense of betrayal and confusion.

Christ's words were shattering every expectation of what Peter assumed to be the Jewish Messiah's purpose. Everything within him must have rebelled against this idiosyncratic Messiah. He knew Jesus was God. Yet how could God be killed? Jesus' reply must have shaken Peter to the core. "But he (Jesus) turned, and said unto Peter, Get thee behind me, Satan: thou art an offence unto me: for thou savor not the things that be of God, but those that be of men." (Matthew 16:23).

We now know, from the clearer perspective of subsequent events, that Peter was arguing—using the false data of human reasoning—against something that simply *resembled* a betrayal. He could not have known then to what extent Christ's death, burial and resurrection would be of incalculable benefit to mankind.

As I considered this account, I began to examine the depth of my own commitment. What were my reactions in the face of seemingly contradictory evidence of God's faithful character and trustworthiness? Did I indeed always trust God *implicitly*? Had I attached unspoken qualifications—or any reservations—to my devotion?

"I will love You unless…?"

"I will serve You but…?"

"I will commit to You until…?"

Out of these musings arose a question that felt almost brutal in its searching intensity, yet one that nevertheless demanded an answer.

"Would I be willing to follow Jesus unconditionally, even when it appeared as if He had betrayed me?"

REASSESSMENT

"Not that I am (I think) in much danger of ceasing to believe in God. The real danger is of coming to believe such dreadful things about Him. The conclusion I dread is not, 'So there's no God after all,' but 'So this is what God's really like. Deceive yourself no longer.'"

—C.S. Lewis

"Self-pity, self-love, fear of suffering, withdrawal from the cross: these are some of the manifestations of the soul life, for its prime motivation is self-preservation. It is exceedingly reluctant to endure any loss."

—Watchman Nee

W*hy must mankind suffer?* Individuals have pondered that question for eons. That question also raises many others. "What is the purpose of suffering?" "If God is love, why does He allow suffering?" and "How should one react to suffering?"

At the root of many of these types of questions is often a deep-seated anguish at the apparent senselessness of it all. If suffering has no meaning—if it serves no discernable purpose—then what is the point? Suffering and trials are generally so pervasive as to be almost completely unexceptional. They are as prosaic and prevalent as dirt.

Such were my despairing views in the early days of loss. Suffering had in effect rendered me commonplace and thereby irrelevant. Car wrecks should not happen to faithful Christians. The accident had reduced a formerly precious and sacrosanct mother and child experience to little more than an insignificant statistic. How could I ever go on unless some sense could be made of the tragedy?

Mankind, enmeshed as we are in the deceitfulness of appearances, seeks answers in obvious places. Simplistic explanations for human suffering abound. Suffering exists because there is no God. Natural laws, when broken, create consequences. Chance and fate rule the day. Karmic influences prevail. Fatalists would chalk up life's angst to little more than some sort of pointless and sadistic cosmic joke. C. S. Lewis facetiously sums up such specious views: ". . . all life will turn out in the end to have been a transitory and senseless contortion upon the idiotic face of infinite matter." This aphorism would hold true if no point could be found in the seemingly pointless.

Yet, the concept of life as a capricious roll of the dice runs counter to all that is distinctly Christian. Believers are to embrace hope, not nihilistic despair. Rejecting glib answers, Christians must, conversely, weigh suffering in view of what we think we know of a kind and loving God. Therein lies the difficulty. For what do we really know of God? Prior to this, I had only experienced Him as a kind and gentle entity. One who had lovingly sent a Savior to rescue me from a terrible destiny. He was, to me, a figure of unimpeachable benevolence—the very soul of goodness. In light of what I had experienced, it seemed I now had to redefine Him.

To find our way forward, what do we do? Retrace our steps to discover what went wrong? Learn from our experiences or the experiences of others?

Someone once suggested, “When you’ve lost your way, go back to the beginning.” Much easier said than done. Finding the beginning by retracing early steps seemed too painful and a means by which the blame game could become the loudest voice. Some insight might be gained by locating where things went wrong, yet who would wish to go back and relive the past with its mistakes and failings? The better approach was to forge a new beginning. But how and where to make that beginning?

Consulting experience to seek wisdom seemed the wrong way around. Contrary to popular belief, experience is not the best teacher. Experience may be the fair teacher in the temporal world, but it’s an insufficient guide to the spiritual one. Experience involves looking backward, which Christians should wisely avoid. Remember Lot’s wife. In fact, hindsight can be cruel. Experience is far too one-dimensional to consult. It does not, in the end, lead to increased wisdom because it reflects what we already know, not what we don’t know. Unfortunately, what we don’t know is what hurts us most. Experience is only validated to the degree that God is welcomed there; it is, however, not a reliable guide. In the end, we must reject experience for the faulty gauge that it represents; it has never been the workings of the human experience or even observation of the natural world that brought mankind to a recognition of God. Externals do not address what ails us. Rather, we find answers to our questions by looking deep within.

I know this because my own relationship with God did not evolve from externals. Although a number of external factors—sermons, books, conversations, relationships–contributed to my becoming aware that a different type of life existed and was desirable, my conversion was based primarily upon unseen, internal factors. It was a hunger, more a starvation, actually, that drove me inexorably to Him. Research and rumination, questionings, yearnings, and an active conscience were far more instrumental in bringing me to a gradual belief in the existence of God than any circumstances that originated from without.

Externals do not address what ails us. Rather, we find answers to our questions by looking deep within.

Since experience did not lead me to God, an experience—though one most terrible—must not now be the catalyst that drives me away. Laying aside experience to the extent that I can, I will instead reexamine what I think I know, or thought I knew of God.

REDEFINING THE GOODNESS OF GOD

"Perfect goodness can never debate about the end to be attained, and perfect wisdom cannot debate about the means most suited to achieve it."

— C.S. Lewis

In order to gain a deeper understanding of the character of God in relation to suffering, I would have to first define what I imagine goodness to be. I will say ahead of time that I would rather doubt my own conceptions of goodness and hold them up to critique rather than heedlessly disparage the goodness of God. If I would presume to accuse God or His motives of being anything less than good, I must first clarify what I think I mean by the concept of good or be in error from the outset.

I might begin by equating goodness with love. We speak of love as the apex, the ultimate virtue. Yet, it is quite possible for love to become something other than good. An inordinate love of drink is not goodness by any stretch, nor is excessive love in a misguided romance.

Kindness may also sometimes appear to be good, and in most cases is, but what happens when an act of kindness—such as lying to spare someone's feelings—becomes a cruelty?

Freedom from pain may seem like an ultimate good. We would like to imagine a world with no pain at all. Yet this too is unrealistic when we consider how pain can be useful—the discomfort of fever driving out the disease for instance—and thereby transformed from something injurious into an irrefutable good.

How does God then view goodness? Can goodness be recognized absent its counterpart? The worldview defines good and evil in earthly terms, as dichotomies. God may well regard these terms—goodness at least—in an altogether different light. Perhaps God considers a desirable end—a gargantuan growth in character generated through tragedy, for instance—sufficient to justify a horror of a means. Such actions would seem utterly heartless of God unless He foresaw a greater good that is not immediately discernible to the sufferer. Is it possible that God is far more interested in our character development than our level of comfort and the process by which He attains that end He considers the ultimate good? When He says, "Be ye therefore perfect, even as your Father which is in Heaven is perfect" (Matthew 5:48), and we know that perfection is beyond our reach, could God, in actuality, be stating His intention to work within us to make a semblance of that happen, come what may?

Is it possible that God is far more interested in our character development than our level of comfort and the process by which He attains that end He considers the ultimate good?

Absent further revelation, however, suffering's purpose remains obscure. We are on this earth and bombarded by sensations and thought processes, the purpose of which is to keep our focus on the here and now. Yet, a recurring theme throughout scripture is that the effects of suffering are intended to transcend the immediate. One intriguing viewpoint is presented in Paul Billheimer's book *Destined for the Throne*. The author defines life on earth as a deliberately planned preparation for life in eternity. He describes our existence as on-the-job training for a future destiny yet to be revealed.

In this interpretation, God is characterized as a wise parent raising stalwart offspring capable of engendering uncommon acts of goodness. In the hands of God, the sufferer gains empathy for fellow sufferers and through hardships, is forged into an individual of extraordinary strength. Thus, a dual purpose is accomplished; the believer becomes both exponentially useful on earth and exceptionally well suited for heaven.

That viewpoint finds its parallel in the human experience. For what parent or teacher does not strive to encourage good character and a sense of accomplishment in their young charges? When a child experiences adversity, or a setback, he or she is admonished to get up and keep going. Strength, independence, and determination are considered admirable reactions to hardship; the traits gained *are* the desired outcome. The purpose is to enhance a child's suitability for life and affect their successful transition into adulthood.

Taking the point to the extreme, what manner of parent would permit, much less plan the torture and agonizing death of their own child? Only the One who saw in Christ the end from the beginning and could envision a greater good that so vastly eclipsed the insufferable pain of the moment that it transcended the experience itself.

When such a magnificent outcome ensues, the suffering is effectually rendered harmless to the extent that the event itself is not only endurable but—well beyond that—considered desirable.

Although I will concede the point that part of God's plan in my loss could be to build or refine my character, that strategy surely represents only a mere fraction of the complete picture. Many pieces are still missing, and one significant piece in particular. The apostle Paul states in 2 Corinthians 1:3-4, "Praise be to God . . . who comforts us in all our troubles, so that we can comfort those in any trouble with the comfort we ourselves receive from God" (NIV). If my usefulness to serve is reliant upon my receiving comfort, and if God seems far less interested than I in maintaining my level of comfort, to whom then do I turn for comfort?

REGAINING PERSPECTIVE

"Suffering, failure, loneliness, sorrow, discouragement, and death will be part of your journey, but the Kingdom of God will conquer all these horrors. No evil can resist grace forever."

—BRENNAN MANNING

If I ascend up into heaven, thou art there: if I make my bed in hell, behold, thou art there.

— PSALM 139:8

"If you're going through hell, keep going."

—WINSTON CHURCHILL

Every person is going to live forever, either in one place or another. That is the Christian viewpoint. It is the frame of reference by which we make judgments on the manner in which we conduct our lives. In the light of that belief, God's laws materially affect how we live, what we do, and how we think during our lifetimes on earth. If we lived to ourselves for only a vapor of a lifespan and then ceased to exist, that would be another matter altogether. Perhaps it would then be immaterial how we acted. Under those circumstances, "Eat, drink, for tomorrow we die" might be an appropriate credo. In both contexts, the beliefs of the adherents to either point of view would undoubtedly lead to immensely divergent standards of behavior.

Christians are not given the license to act in any manner in which they please. They must seriously grapple with the knowledge that every decision to act or think in a certain way has a counterpart in the spiritual world. The fact that we will one day give account to a holy God is a sobering reality juxtaposed against the prevailingly laissez-faire worldview that paints a picture of God as either a non-existent figment or a grandfatherly figure of senile beneficence. We are vastly mistaken when we assume that He merely winks, turns a blind eye, or shrugs His shoulders at our highly corrupt and self-willed shenanigans.

An ongoing danger to believers is the inclination to remain in the moment and lose sight of—or choose to disregard—the eternal perspective. It is tempting to go astray when stuck as we are in a temporal body subjected to all manner of physical sensations and mentally assaulted with incessant, largely unreliable, yet immensely convincing stimuli. Preserving a godly perspective is no simple matter. This I know. The cacophony of grief created a derailment of sorts; I am, after all, only human, and it took longer for me to regain a heavenly perspective than to initially attain one. In this extremity, a tremendous source of encouragement came from reading the accounts of other Christians, fellow sufferers, who struggled to overcome adversity and went on to live in victory and with inspired purpose.

A landmark moment in my journey back to faith was generated by an account shared by Joni Eareckson Tada. A quadriplegic "bolted to a chair" for 40 years, she took exception to the scriptural description of her sufferings as a "light affliction" as described in 2 Corinthians 4:17. A confrontation with God she describes in her book, *Heaven: Your Real Home*, reflects the agonized cry of her heart.

"Stuck in a wheelchair and staring out the window over the field of our farm, I wondered, *Lord how in the world can You consider my troubles light and momentary? I will never walk or run again. I will never use my hands . . . I'm trapped in front of this window. Maybe You see all of this achieving an eternal glory, but all I see is one awful day after the next of life in this stinking wheelchair!*"

Years later, Tada realized that the only thing that could outweigh the pain of a permanent paralysis was the counterbalance of the weight of an eternal gain. She called that perspective an "end-of-time" view. Her affliction only became "light" in view of its temporary nature. Her belief that God would ultimately put an end to all suffering—and make all things beautiful in His time—enabled her to move forward.

Our pain is proportionately eased to the degree that we understand the truth about eternal gains.

To this day, she endures with joy. Her faith continues to inspire me to look beyond circumstances to a future far different from my current experience. If she, in her great suffering could bear it bravely with the help of God, so indeed I, in my less severe trial, could also do. Our pain is proportionately eased to the degree that we understand the truth about eternal gains.

William Tyndale was a leading figure in the Reformation whose translation of the New Testament (and part of the Old) from Greek and Hebrew was taken as a direct challenge to the hegemony of English law and the church. He was jailed and subsequently martyred for his heretical belief in the justification of the Christian by faith and not by works. He penned this admonishment to the believer and soon after paid the ultimate price of obeying God rather than man.

"If God promises riches, the way thereto is poverty. Whom he loveth, him he chasteneth: whom he exalteth, he casteth down: whom he saveth, he damneth first. He bringeth no man to heaven, except he send him to hell first."

This sentiment, despite its severity, could well be the truest portrayal of the correct perspective. Though meant to be taken figuratively rather than literally—obviously,

God sends no one to hell, we, in effect, send ourselves—it is much closer to reality than what we have been led to believe.

We must remember that God's intention in trials is not just to shape us in His image, but also to lead us through the trials and on to victory. To stop short of a triumphant outcome is to settle for less than God's best.

> *"Now thanks be unto God Who always causes us to triumph in Christ..."*
>
> **(2 Corinthians 2:14)**

RELINQUISHING FALSE EXPECTATIONS

"Let me assure you, this [sanctification] is not attained, save through pain, weariness and labor; and it will be reached by a path that will wonderfully disappoint your expectations."

—JEANNE MARIE BOUVIER DE LA MOTTE GUYON

"We can be deceived by believing what is untrue, but we certainly are also deceived by not believing what is true."

—SOREN KIERKEGAARD

I was badly misled. I now perceive that for years I'd been laboring under an egregious misconception regarding the life of faith. A presupposition, constructed in minuscule, barely detectable increments over a considerable period of time had become deeply embedded in my psyche. The presupposition was the deceptive premise that I could experience a life devoid of most, if not all, suffering as long as I had enough faith.[2] That an expectation so utterly antithetical to the actual teachings of Christ could become any Christian's modus operandi is troubling. That it had undeniably become mine, shocks me still. An epic *pons asinorum*[3] added to an already lengthy list.

From where did this expectation of a life without suffering evolve? Did not Christ make it clear that in this world, we would have tribulation? Wasn't it He who stated that "The servant is not greater than His master." (John 15:20); that if He was persecuted, so would we also be? He is the original, and we the derivative. Whose word then should carry more weight? Whose experience should we deem the most authentic? Yet, in the face of innumerable scriptural injunctions and warnings for believers to expect, prepare for, and yes, even embrace trials and sufferings as

---

[2] By faith I mean actions, thoughts, words, and beliefs carried out in accordance with scriptural principles.

[3] A problem that severely tests the ability of an inexperienced person.

the "cost to be counted" (Luke 14:28), Christians persist in expending their faith to increase their own level of comfort.

My panic-stricken reaction to the various trials I'd encountered were evidence that my expectations and, consequently, my ability to cope with the unexpected were hopelessly out of skew with reality. When the battle came, I was woefully outgunned, left traumatized and wondering how such things could have possibly come to pass. What had happened to me? I knew the scriptures and could quote them at will; I'd spent years studying them in depth. My prayer life was a tremendous source of joy. Teaching the basic elements of the faith to new believers was my great privilege and my pleasure. How had I been led astray?

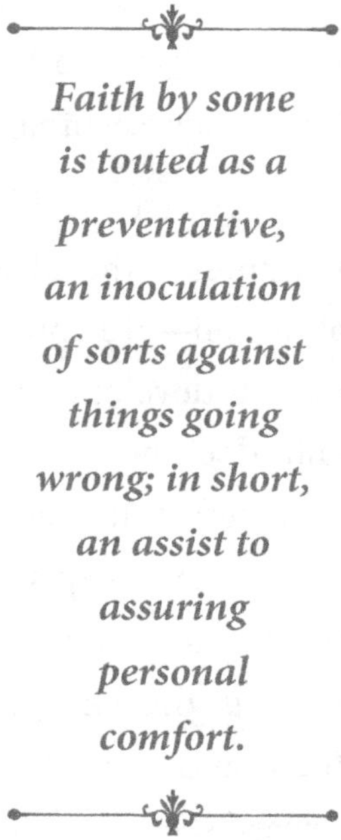

In analyzing some of the many sermons and teachings on faith promulgated by popular gospel ministers, I noticed a common refrain among them. Faith by some is touted as a preventative, an inoculation of sorts against things going wrong; in short, an assist to assuring personal comfort. The emphasis on self decidedly eclipses in importance the need to expend our faith on behalf of others, to help the helpless in a lost and dying world. Rather than denying self, as represented by Christ's teaching, this doctrine instead panders to it.

Personal health, wealth, safety, happiness—the absence of suffering above all—are considered indications of well-developed faith. This pseudo-faith doctrine of "comfort Christianity" is a zero-sum game carried out by wolves in sheep's clothing who are playing for keeps. What they hope to keep is the enraptured attention of their audience. Celebrity status and immense financial reward seem to follow those who tickle the "itching ears" (2 Timothy 4:3) of the hearers. Any teachings on suffering then would be anathema to their carefully crafted message. Suffering has thus become the sour note in the chorus of comfort Christianity.

Suffering has thus become the sour note in the chorus of comfort Christianity.

I did not purposefully buy into these presumptions to any great extent, but time spent as a congregate under this type of teaching inevitably resulted in a gradual inculcation to their perverse message. It is human nature to intentionally believe only what we wish to, and I was certainly not immune. I'd hoped the wishful-thinking-way-of-faith was true. I found it was not, and my faith was nearly shipwrecked as a result.

The truth is that suffering is not to be avoided at all costs but rather to be embraced. Christians are continuously to be undergoing a process of self-denial and sanctification [purification]. Not in the manner one would expect—in penance and self-flagellation—but rather in our daily decisions to follow God's commands, even those we deem uncomfortable.

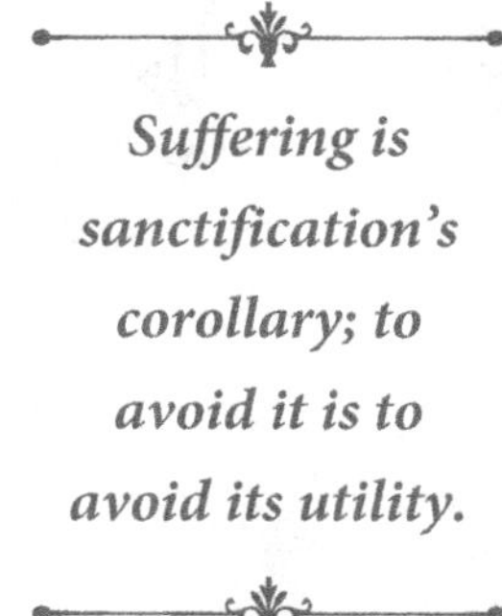

Suffering is sanctification's corollary; to avoid it is to avoid its utility. In essence, when we dodge suffering, we forsake the best opportunity to become more like the God we serve. During trials, when we are forced to depend more on God and less on ourselves, His power and strength within us increases correspondingly. When we choose to voluntarily submit our will to His, something extraordinary occurs. Rather than disappear as a personality, we become the best version of ourselves.

To launch out from a place of relative comfort and safety is difficult. Working the works of Christ involves sacrifice and self-denial. The words of the apostle Paul, found in 2 Corinthians 11:23-28, provide an accurate depiction of the cost of living by faith:

> *23 Are they servants of Christ? (I am out of my mind to talk like this.) I am more. I have worked much harder, been in prison more frequently, been flogged more severely, and been exposed to death again and again. 24 Five times I received from the Jews the forty lashes minus one. 25 Three times I was beaten with rods, once I was pelted with stones, three times I was shipwrecked, I spent a night and a day in the open sea, 26 I have been constantly on the move. I have been in danger from rivers, in danger from bandits, in danger from my fellow Jews, in danger from Gentiles; in danger in the city, in danger in the country, in danger at*

sea; and in danger from false believers. 27 I have labored and toiled and have often gone without sleep; I have known hunger and thirst and have often gone without food; I have been cold and naked. 28 Besides everything else, I face daily the pressure of my concern for all the churches.

(NIV)

Is it any wonder that Christ warned us that "narrow is the way… and few there be that find it?" (Matthew 7:13-14) This is the authentic life of faith. We need to stop pretending that it's not true.

RESOLVING THE "WHY?"

Those who love their life lose it, and those who hate their life in this world will keep it for eternal life.

— John 12:25

You're born. You suffer. You die. Fortunately, there's a loophole.

— Billy Graham

The secret things belong unto the Lord our God: but those things which are revealed belong unto us and to our children forever.

— Deuteronomy 29:29

Many parents can relate to the dilemma they face when their child asks the inevitable question,

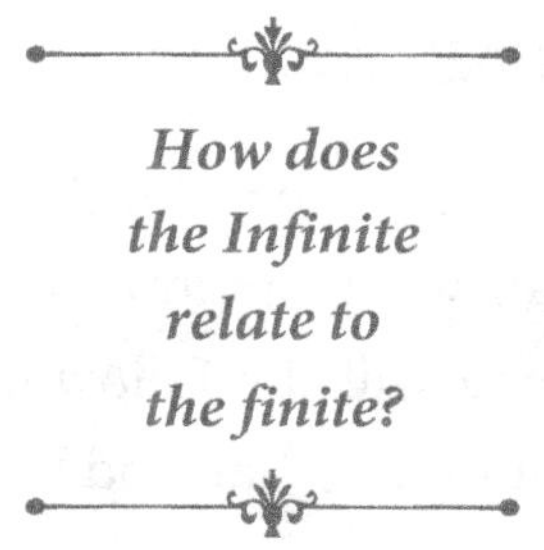

"Why?" The more sensitive among us remember the frustration we felt as children when our parents would respond with an exasperating, "Because I said so," for it was by no means a satisfactory answer in the least. At that moment, with the question "Why?" dangling in midair between parent and child, we realize that we face a point of decision, whether to try and explain the unexplainable to a child who could not possibly understand an answer far beyond the scope of their years and experience or to deliver a fatwa as reply.

This, in a nutshell, represents God's ongoing reality. How does the Infinite relate to the finite? Although He is not answerable to any of us, God—in a similar manner in which He shows restraint to properly relate to the human condition—graciously provides answers to the most compelling lifelong questions that we will ever face. We need not look to our circumstances or go to any great lengths to seek out these answers, for they have already been provided to us in general terms through the instrument of

God's Word.[4]

You may think this a disappointingly over-simplistic answer to an immensely complicated issue, but consider, if you will the following points that address the "Why?" of suffering that God has taken pains to elucidate in scripture.

The greatest scourge to mankind is death. Yet contrary to what we may have been taught, God is not the author of death. Human beings were never meant to experience death. Death came as a result of the fall of man as described in Romans 5:12:

> *"...just as through one man sin entered the world, and death through sin, in this way death came to all people..."*

[4] These points are elucidated in generalities, not specifics. Specifics particular to our circumstances are not necessarily found verbatim in scripture, but can be revealed to us as individuals, both through the Logos (written word) and the Rhema (spoken word). God answered many questions regarding my daughter's passing, the answers of which were both highly individualized and deeply personal.

According to scripture, death will ultimately be done away with. This is stated in 1 Corinthians 15:26:

> *"The last enemy to be destroyed is death."*

In the meantime, we need to take care not to attribute all matters of death and dying to God. In John 10:10, Jesus stated this:

> *"The thief comes only to steal and kill and destroy; I have come that they may have life and have it to the full."*

If the Father is in the killing business and the Son is in the healing business, they effectively become a house divided. We know the identity of the thief, and it is not God. But the murderer is also clearly identified in scripture. In John 8:44, Jesus called the devil "…a murderer from the beginning." In view of these truths, we are left with a puzzling dichotomy. Perhaps God does not *cause* death, but does He *allow* it?

Throughout scripture there are passages that are written either in the causative sense or the permissive sense.

When dealing with matters of life and death, we need to distinguish one sense from the other. Most of the time God's actions are in the permissive sense, and we jump to the conclusion that an all-powerful God could have stopped the course of nature. Although we may believe that God has not deliberately caused the death of our loved ones, we need to understand the background of God's alleged "permissive" attributes. This raises the ubiquitous question, "Who is actually running things?

Many question how a good God could have made such a mess of this world. A scripture found in 2 Corinthians 4:4 provides insight that corrects this presupposition:

> *"In their case the god of this world has blinded the minds of the unbelievers, to keep them from seeing the light of the gospel of the glory of Christ, who is the image of God."*

Notice the lower case "g" in the word "god." Who then is this god of the lower-case g? An incident that occurred during Christ's temptation in the wilderness provides the answer.

> *And the devil taking Him (Jesus) up into a high mountain, showed him all the kingdoms of the world in a moment of time. And the devil said unto Him, "All this authority I will give you, and their glory,* ***for this has been delivered to me, and I give it to whomever I wish.*** *If you will worship me, all will be Yours."*
>
> LUKE 4: 5-7 (NKJV)

Surprisingly, Jesus did not challenge the devil's statement. Why not? Who gave satan the right to call the things of the world his? If he was lying, and the kingdoms of the world were not his to give, then the offer would not have been a temptation for Jesus. The point is clear. God may own the world, but the world's system is under entirely different management.

Who then, handed this power over to the dark side? In a word…us. Mankind, since the dawn of time, has chosen evil over good and set in motion forces that are unimaginably difficult to deal with. Humanity has become unwitting pawns in a struggle between dark and light.

We are at war. According to scripture, mankind is engaged in a war, but not one comprised of actual battles for bits of territory, but for the far weightier spoil of an eternal destiny. We face an onslaught by unseen forces against our bodies, our wills, our minds, and our emotions in an all-or-nothing war for the human soul. A passage in Ephesians 6:12 provides a vivid description of our situation.

> *For ours is not a conflict with mere flesh and blood, but with the despotisms, the empires,* ***the forces that control and govern this dark world****--the spiritual hosts of evil arrayed against us in the heavenly warfare.*
>
> (WEYMOUTH)

In this conflict, every rule of engagement is upended. Hague and Geneva Conventions and Protocols are nonexistent. Our foe considers everyone fair game for attack—including the sick, wounded, shipwrecked, and imprisoned. In this war, no bystander is considered innocent and collateral damage is commonplace. Soldiers are singled out for particular brutality.

Targeted by a system that is being run by nefarious forces, it should therefore come as no surprise to us when one of ours becomes a casualty of war. When we enlist in God's army, we do so, understanding fully the risks we run. God warns us to count the cost (Luke 14:28). He also warns us not to consider it.

Did my daughter's fearless witness for Jesus Christ make her a target? Perhaps. Aligning my life with the Lord's, and encouraging her to do so as well, may have put her earthly life at risk. Yet would we not determinedly run that risk again to ensure that in the end, our loved ones would be tucked up, forever safe, in their Savior's arms? We know we would. The alternative to living the Christian life—and dying without a Savior—is unthinkable. Spending eternity apart from God is the worst death imaginable. If my loved one had to be taken, so be it. My daughter was the Lord's and was dedicated to His service from the outset. Our children and family members are not "ours." They are on loan; we do not own them.

Another factor presented in scripture addresses part of the "Why?" of certain events. Mankind has been afforded complete freedom of choice. Both good and bad outcomes are set in motion by the choices we make. Our free will is something that God categorically refuses to control. His fellowship with mankind is eventuated with willing servants, not slaves.

Good parents model their parenting after the workings of our Heavenly Father. What parent would prefer raising their children with brute force? Wise parents encourage their progeny to make good choices, think independently, and develop critical thinking skills. This is accomplished though intelligent guidance and allowing children to make their own mistakes along the way.

In that same manner, God places the onus on us to choose properly, and when we do not, there are always consequences, some more dire than others. An untimely death, a terrible illness, natural disasters, and every manner of abuse and injustice are indications of a hideously fallen world energized by mankind's freedom of choice. Our choices have created most of this mess, yet it's often the innocent who suffer.

We also must consider the reality of the laws of nature. Violating these laws, either accidentally or deliberately, always creates consequences. You jump off a roof and you break a leg. To make matters worse, we live in a corrupt environment. Our gene pool has become polluted through genetic experimentation. Our denatured food and fouled water sources speak of the obvious effects of humans' unconsidered actions. We have yet to walk in full maturity in our stewardship of one another and God's creation.

Christ frequently superseded natural law to bless individuals. He healed the sick, raised the dead, commanded the sea, and turned water into wine. His Highest Will and His best for us was demonstrated in His earthly walk. It is not God's desire to have us live as victims of circumstances. Yet many of God's children have fallen victim to the whims of nature which run the gamut from dreaded diseases to natural disasters.

The early church fathers knew something about walking in the miraculous. I will venture to say that what was available to them should be with us now. Is it not written that,

> *"Jesus Christ is the same yesterday, and today and forever?"*
>
> **(HEBREWS 13:8)**

But only a very few fully grasp their rights and privileges provided through Christ, with the result that many suffer unnecessarily.

Is it possible, then, that we all have a part to play in offsetting some of the tragedies in this world? We must at least consider the fact that the church has only partially fulfilled the Great Commission as presented in Mark 16:15-18:

> *And he said unto them, Go ye into all the world, and preach the gospel to every creature. He that believeth and is baptized shall be saved; but he that believeth not shall be damned.* ***And these signs shall follow them that believe; In my name shall they cast out devils; they shall speak with new tongues; They shall take up serpents; and if they drink any deadly thing, it shall not hurt them; they shall lay hands on the sick, and they shall recover.***

Indeed, where are the "greater works" that Jesus promised would be taking place through the church as mentioned in John 14:12?

> *"Most assuredly, I say to you, he who believes in Me, the works that I do he will do also; and greater works than these he will do, because I go to My Father.*

Consequently, we can conclude that some of the world's suffering, and the responsibility for alleviating it, can, in part, be laid at the feet of a church that is not aware of her latent power. Will there ever come a day when the church rises up and takes her rightful place as the channel for the miracles of God? Or will we continue to insist that the age of miracles has passed? In maintaining this, we err in the same manner described in Hosea 4:6:

> *"My people are destroyed for lack of knowledge."*

Finally, it may help us come to terms with loss when we recognize that what the enemy meant for harm, can ultimately be turned to good. In Genesis 50:20, Joseph, who was sold into slavery by his own brothers, states this:

> *"You intended to harm me, but God intended it for good to accomplish what is now being done, the saving of many lives."*

We also find in scripture a promise that heartens us even when the worst has happened. The scripture is found in Romans 8:28:

> *"And we know that all things work together to those who love God, to those who are called according to his purpose."*

How exactly does this work? Every promise in scripture has the potential to be unleashed when appropriated by faith. We must believe that it will be so, despite all evidence to the contrary. Christians are admonished to react to all of life's trials by exercising our faith. It might be argued that our commandment to gain maturity in Christ is sufficient justification for the *"Why?"* of trials.

Indeed, Christians flourish to the extent that we overcome circumstances. We are admonished to endeavor to be *independent* of circumstances, and to strive to remain content regardless of what we are facing (Philippians 4:11). The task is impossible through any normal means. In fact, the only way to truly accomplish this is to die.

The apostle Paul states, "I die daily" (1 Corinthians 15:31). Yet in what sense did he "die?" Paul considered himself dead to the effects of trials and sin. Dying to self is one of the core themes of scripture. Christ's beautiful prayer in the Garden of Gethsemane, "Not my will but Thine be done" (Luke 22:42), and His willingness to

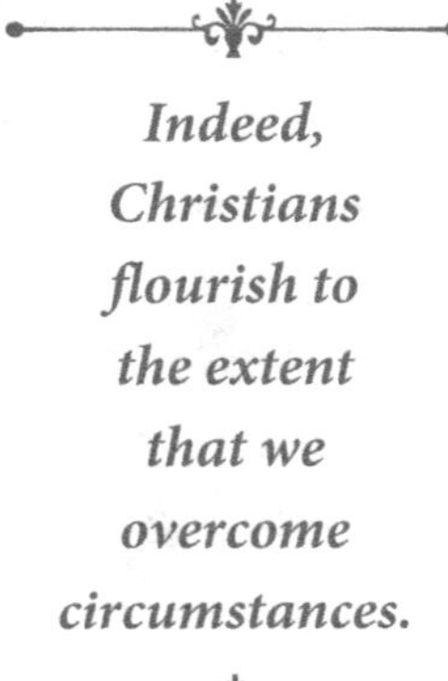

voluntarily lay down His life exemplifies the keystone of the Christian faith. In volunteering to die to our own will—our actions, dreams, and desires—and receiving in their stead God's will in our daily lives, we are following in Christ's steps. As we choose to "lay down our lives" in our daily obedience we, in effect, "die."

As the apostle Paul states in Galatians 2:20:

> *"I am crucified with Christ, nevertheless I live; yet not I, but Christ lives in me: and the life which I now live in the flesh I live by the faith of the Son of God, who loved me, and gave himself for me."*

Paul's death to self made him alive unto God. His complete identification with Christ, both in suffering and service, rendered Paul virtually impervious to the ups and downs of life. Living in an attitude of "surrender" is a privilege and a choice afforded to every believer.

Reckoning oneself as dead creates the capacity to maintain calm during chaos, to trust when it appears that all is lost, and to remain unmoved and unshakable when all has been shaken. After all, what hurt or pain can afflict a dead man?

I was able to move forward to the extent that I was willing to release the things of this world, including the loss of my child, in order to fully embrace God's plan for my life. It was an impossible task to accomplish on my own and only achievable through Christ. When we prayerfully, and by an act of our will, offer ourselves to God daily—as Paul states in Romans 12:1:

> *"I beseech you therefore, brethren, by the mercies of God, that you present your bodies a living sacrifice, holy, acceptable to God, which is your reasonable service."*

—we become one with God's purpose. In essence, we begin to experience life on a different level, viewed through the lens of eternity.

As stated in Colossian 3:3:

> *"For you died, and your life is now hidden with Christ in God."*

To be "dead" then, is to be truly free.

CHAPTER 3

THE WAY FORWARD

ACCESSING THE COMFORTER

"The Son of God is the Teacher of men, giving to them of his Spirit—that Spirit which manifests the deep things of God, being to a man the mind of Christ. The great heresy of the Church of the present day is unbelief in this Spirit."

—GEORGE MACDONALD

In our childhood, my sisters and I were experts at pitting one parent against the other. If mom said no, rather than take no for an answer, we would immediately run to dad, and vice versa. At any particular moment, at least one parent could be counted on to be in a better mood than the other and be, therefore, more lenient. That disingenuous trick began to backfire as our parents became wise to us, and we eventually had to give up trying to manipulate them for our shamefully self-serving purposes.

During my estrangement from God, when we were barely on speaking terms—as "Father" in this case had unquestionably become to me a great mystery—I felt there was nowhere and no one to turn to for comfort. If God had allowed the pain, I reasoned, He could hardly be the panacea for the pain. With every dream seemingly denied in a resounding "No!" I was desperate to receive some glimmer of leniency, some version of a divinely relenting "Yes!" Not knowing what else to do, I delved more deeply into the scriptures, searching for the God I used to know, hoping to find something—perhaps a dimension of Him—that I could relate to. My search led to a study of the Trinity and, through that, the discovery of the fullest and best response I could ever have received to my request for comfort.

The concept of the Trinity, three Gods in one, is a theological sticking point in the minds of many. The notion of three entities functioning as one may seem to some an idiosyncratic idea at best, or at the least, an absurd implausibility. Yet, this conception of deity is not so far-fetched when one considers that every human being is the perfect mimicry of this arrangement. Serving as the model, the Trinity is comprised of the Father, the great "soul" of the universe, the Holy Spirit, the eternal Spirit of a holy God, and the Son, who is God manifested in bodily form.[5]

In like manner, mankind possesses a soul (a mind, a will, and emotions) and we have an eternal spirit, both of which are housed in a body. Dispensing with the fiction that we could manage perfectly fine as disembodied spirits floating around in a concrete world, we must concede that God's arrangement is very well thought out. Each one of the three factions could not possibly function without the others; and all three working in concert create a beautifully balanced individual.

The separate nature of each member of the Trinity is clearly denoted in the scriptures. The Father is the unquestioned Lord of all and, as Creator, eclipses everything created—in power, wisdom, and strength. I understood God the Father's role well enough to reverence and, at times, fear Him. The Son, as much God as the

[5] An obvious simplification for the sake of illustration.

Father, is the Savior of the world, sent to experience life as a man and pay the ultimate sacrifice to deliver us from our sin. I understood His role quite well. I had personally experienced the saving power of grace in Christ. The Holy Spirit, thoroughly God as well, fulfills a role that to the present day has been surprisingly downplayed—and even at times completely ignored—by believers no less. This has been to our enormous detriment. I was soon to learn firsthand how precious His role could be.

When Jesus was nearing the end of His earthly ministry, He communicated several final essential concepts to His staff. These instructions are found in the Gospel of John, chapters 14-16. Knowing what He was about to suffer and understanding exactly how his disciples would react—and what, indeed, their lives would become after His demise—He thought it imperative to apprise them of the role and purpose of the Person designated to act as His substitute on earth. As radical an idea as this may seem, Jesus, with the Father, had arranged for a stand-in!

The person of the Holy Spirit—Who is indeed a person, not a disembodied ghost—is the fulfillment of Christ's promise to send another Comforter who would stay with us forever. The extraordinary fact of the matter is that Jesus emphasized the necessity of His own departure ("*...it is* ***expedient*** *for you that I go away" John 16:7*) in order to make room for the arrival of the Holy Spirit. The profound significance of this action cannot be overemphasized, for it was the Holy Spirit's arrival at Pentecost that ushered in the Church Age.

The Comforter's role is not limited to providing comfort. The Holy Spirit's role, as fleshed out in Christ's landmark sermon, is an expansive one. His role encompasses teaching, comforting, revealing truth, bearing witness of Jesus, glorifying God, reproving the world of sin, righteousness, and judgment, and providing wisdom to the church.

Our multidimensional God is thus equipped to meet every conceivable need of mankind, beginning with salvation, and extending to wisdom, comfort, and strength. Using a worldly and embarrassingly overly simplistic analogy, we could liken the Trinity to a team of teachers, each with a different role but all with necessarily identical aims.

As Comforter, the Holy Spirit's role is unmatched. When I finally understood that I could avail myself of His assistance, I discovered a great source of strength and comfort. During my darkest times, in despair of life, when sorrow overshadowed every good thing, and the pain of separation became hideously palpable—when I could do nothing else to help myself—I learned to call upon Him. He ushered in and revealed God's *Presence,* which was exactly what I needed. I did not need answers, or more coping strategies, or one more thing to *try.* I needed God. The Holy Spirit brought fresh revelations of my Father's love and care for me and continuously pointed me to Jesus.

Whether it was a Presence, a feeling, a *knowing* that all would be well no matter what, I cannot pinpoint even now. I can assert with confidence that the utter sweetness of His fellowship and the steadfast warmth of His reassurances brought me back to my senses. In retrospect, I realize that this was all the Father's doing. Despite my experiencing the worst, He nevertheless provided the best of Himself, His very Spirit, to comfort me. I don't claim to understand how this was possible, but it happened.

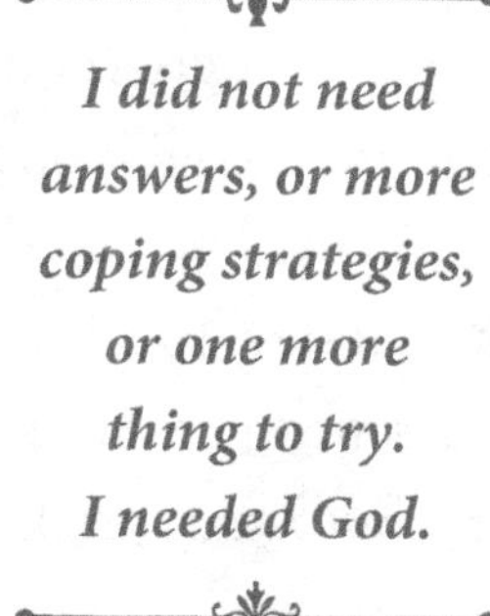
I did not need answers, or more coping strategies, or one more thing to try. I needed God.

PSYCHOLOGY'S FICTIONS

"Psychoanalysis is a confession without absolution."

—C. K. Chesterton

When in the throes of one of the worst seasons of grief, I decided to see a psychiatrist in the hope that they could offer some relief for the suffering. The psychiatrist was a well-qualified Harvard graduate who was kind and reasonably astute. She let me talk uninterrupted for the scheduled hour, presented me with an informational brochure on grief, and sent me on my way with a prescription for a tranquilizer. I appreciated being given the opportunity to vent to someone who was a dispassionate listener. The experience was helpful in that aspect, and thus I wholeheartedly recommend that a bereaved person find someone trustworthy to speak with.

The other resources were less helpful. The prescription went unfilled; I refused the medication, fearing that it would postpone and extend the grieving process.[6] I found the brochure to be personally off-putting because the grief process was pigeonholed into a series of random steps, and the suggestions for grief recovery distilled into a collection of hackneyed homilies. The advice was, to me, singularly unenlightening, if not infuriating. I eventually trashed the pamphlet, but not before taking a good look.

What I found therein were bits of advice—spawned from the behavioral sciences—that, rather than offering comfort, instead had the opposite effect. These sayings' well-intentioned misuse has made me doubt their relevance to any Christian, much less a grieving one. Psychoanalysis generally ignores scriptural principles and as a result, offers very little in the way of authentic counsel or comfort.

To characterize grief as a manageable secession of stages, phases, steps or even to suggest that a "typical" process exists can be deeply unsettling if not insulting to

[6] No judgment intended here; if medication helps you, use it. Always with caution and under the supervision of a physician, of course.

those whose lives have been turned upside-down. Such advice can be particularly offensive to those who have suffered profound loss, such as the loss of an only child, or the loss of more than one child, those who have lost multiple family members or a lifelong companion and so on. I must therefore caution against a wholesale reliance on any bereavement counsel that is not based upon the Word of God. In the end, placing our trust for recovery in any person other than God will undoubtedly lead to disappointment.

That said, I offer here a partial list of what I term "grief's harmful words" presented in no particular order.

Heading the list is the expression to be "*in denial.*" When you've lost a loved one, denial is an outright impossibility. If being in a state of denial represents the utter disbelief one experiences at first learning of a loved one's passing, then we will leave it alone. As to the term's applicability in bereavement, I must take exception. The irreversible changes one undergoes—the loved one's absence, the broadsides of pain in the morning upon awakening, the vain attempts to fill the void, ongoing struggles to cope with waves of sorrow—are on their face proof of a reality that is absolutely undeniable. Regarding the death from cancer of his beloved wife, Joy Davidman, C.S. Lewis had this to say regarding the inexorableness of loss: *"Her death is like the sky; spread all over."* To deny a death, one might as well deny the sunrise.

Another disagreeable term is the ubiquitous expression "*to seek closure.*" It is difficult to understand what exactly is meant by this phrase. Webster's dictionary defines it several different ways, including: to bring to an end, to conclude, to close, an individual's desire for a firm answer to a question, or to be rid of ambiguity. I would question how such closure should be put into effect regarding bereavement? It may connote a wise applicability if one is in a relationship that is not reciprocated and thus warrant closure by some definition. Perhaps closure would be appropriate in a career change, or a move across the country, or cutting one's financial losses. However, it ought to be disqualified for use in circumstances that disallow the option of choice. In the case of the bereaved, there is no choice. How could one choose to close a door that has already been perfunctorily slammed in his or her face?

Invoking the need for closure asks what of the bereaved exactly? To close the door on the memory of a loved one who has died? Close the door on the vicissitudes of the grief experience? Close the door on the relentless thoughts or images or regrets or sorrows? News flash: After many years without my daughter, I will never stop missing her, I will never stop wishing she were here, and I will never cease to mourn her passing. Indeed, why must I? Closure, in any sense of the word in this type of circumstance, is utterly unavailing.

And as to the hope of finding conclusive answers to the questions raised by a loved one's passing—thus eliminating any ambiguities on the subject—there is slim hope of attaining that type of definitive this side of heaven.

Another exceptionally unkind approach is to admonish the bereaved to "*move on*," or "*get over it.*" (and the quicker the better in the opinion of some, as one was overheard commenting regarding me, "*Shouldn't she be over that by now?*") Implying that someone should "move on" connotes asking him or her to leave someone or something behind. This is unthinkable to the bereaved, who would feel their loved one's life devalued or their loss somehow diminished by the act of moving on. Eventually, the grieving will choose to "move forward," for indeed, life goes on. This kinder, and thus infinitely preferable, phrase is of particular value to those who believe their loved one is actually in their future. Looking forward is more easily accomplished by those who understand that time is a continuum, that life on earth is a mere blink, and that eternity is lived each moment. Looking forward gains relevance when considered in terms of "*putting one's hand to the plow...*" (Luke 9:62) and not looking back, but rather ahead.

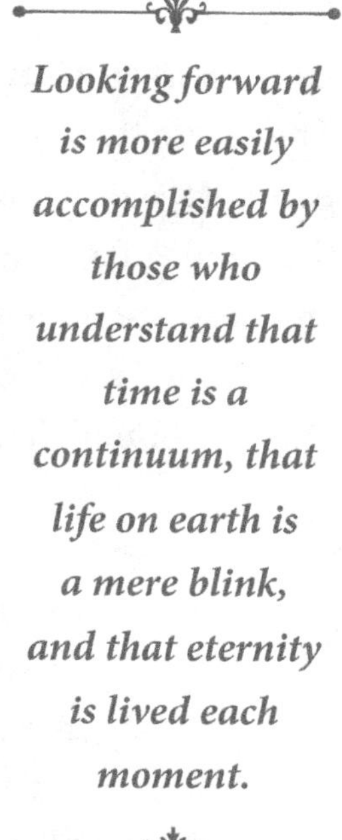
Looking forward is more easily accomplished by those who understand that time is a continuum, that life on earth is a mere blink, and that eternity is lived each moment.

Yet another platitude that creates more questions than answers is the phrase "*letting go.*" This ridiculous cliché offers no clarification regarding what to let go of or even why. Let go of the person? Let go of the past? Should one let go of the memory of a loved one? Forget them utterly? Release them to their eternal rest, evoking a Jonathon

Livingston Seagull New Age platitude, "*If you love someone, set them free?*" Christians need not heed this type of advice. They are better served with an encouragement to place their entire hope of recovery, and past, present, and future, into the hands of a loving heavenly Father. Indeed, things that are past are in God's domain. Ecclesiastes 3:15, reads "…and God seeks again what is past." Referring to this verse Dietrich Bonhoeffer writes:

> *"I suspect that these last words mean that nothing that is past is lost, that God gathers up again with us our past, which belongs to us. So, when we are seized by a longing for the past—and this may happen when we least expect it—we may be sure that it is only one of the many "hours" that God is holding ready for us."* [7]

If God evidently does not let go of the past, then why should we? We may forget the *things* that are behind (read: wrong actions, thoughts, sins, lifestyles) but never the

---

[7] Bonhoeffer, imprisoned for his resistance to the Nazi regime, was mourning the loss of time that should have been spent with his betrothed and his family.

people. Memorializing the lives of those who lived in faith—such as catalogued in Hebrews Chapter 11—affords us deep, rich, and lasting object lessons.

Finally, we are cautioned to avoid glorifying or "*deifying*" those who have passed. This pronouncement represents an inaccuracy. To deify someone means to view him or her worthy of veneration or worship as a god. In this sense, it signals a profound misunderstanding of the bereaved person's viewpoint and the departed one's actuality.

Enlightened people acknowledge their loved ones' imperfections. Yet, in grief, we want to remember what's relevant and lasting about our loved one's lives. Their true selves and their best selves—their very essence—is their spirit. It is not a denial of who they were in all their foursquare reality, but rather a clear-headed recognition of the transcendence of that person's spirit.

The recreated human spirit is the element that matters most, not the mistakes, the failures, or the sin. This, for the Christian, is the "God's-eye view" of all of us. The one who dies in Christ is already free from the constraints of sin in the same way all of those who serve Him will one day be. To view the departed in just that way is to acknowledge reality, not embellish it.

In the final analysis, there is scriptural proof regarding mankind's divinity. It's found in Psalms 82:6. "I have said, ye are ***gods***; and all of you are children of the Most High."

This, in summary, is the best representation of our true standing. Because we were created in the image of God, we hold the spark of the divine.

THE PRIVILEGE OF WORSHIP

"Without worship we go about miserable."

—A. W. Tozer

". . . the hour is coming, and now is, when the true worshipers shall worship the Father in spirit and truth, for the Father seeks such to worship Him"

— John 4:23

Music is intrinsically woven into the very fiber of my being. Since childhood, I've spent many years in the study, practice, and performance of music, at one point seriously considering a career as a pianist. It was, therefore, a telling symptom of the degree of trauma precipitated by Lisa's death that the music just stopped.

Occasionally, I would pick up my guitar and plunk away, but twelve years came and went, and I didn't touch the piano, sing in public, or lead worship in a church setting. Something had happened within to crush the creative flow. Whether it was a rational decision or excuse, I cannot say even now. Nonetheless, the talent—even the inclination to do anything about it—lay dormant and virtually extinguished.

I have always been very aware of the importance of music—its usefulness in worship in particular—in elevating a believer out of their current experience into thrilling realms of unity with God. I have experienced firsthand that transfiguring rapture enough to know its worth. Yet, for a time, the gift existed in lock down. While miming the words in a worship service, my heart remained disengaged. Although listening to worship music provided a great source of solace, participating in it had become another matter altogether. For a season at least, the most I could muster was to sit there doing nothing but allowing the music to wash over me. That was sufficient for a good long while. It was only later that God began to require a bit more of me.

God has provided believers with tools to help us navigate the Christian life. Among them are prayer, the written Word, fellowship, service, and worship. Although we often rank it lower in importance than the other tools, worship is not optional for the Christian. In fact, scripture commands us to praise God even when to do so involves great sacrifice.

As documented repeatedly in scriptural accounts, true worship engenders spectacular effects. Because God inhabits the praises of His people, worship guarantees His appearance. During worship, God delivers instructions and alters circumstances to the point of superseding natural law if necessary. That God uses these sessions of worship to fellowship with us is a truth of immense import when we consider how gracious a gesture from how mighty a source! In His presence reside treasures of matchless joy, rest, and refreshment. Prior to losing my daughter, I had often availed myself of this privilege to my enormous advantage. But therein lay the difficulty.

I reasoned that in those times in the past when the presence of God was tangible, so close He could be *felt,* when the voice of instruction and comfort flowed with the crystal clarity and stunning beauty of a vibrant stream, why then did He not speak to me of what was to come? After all, God had ample opportunities then to forewarn me or prepare me, or more to the point, tell me how to prevent this terrible thing from happening. In these moments when He had my full attention, when things of earth had dimmed to the point where not much that was material mattered, I could have perhaps been told the worst and yet still found the strength to endure.

Instead, the God in whom I trusted with my whole heart had remained strangely and unyieldingly silent. My heart began to misgive me; for now, I doubted the authenticity of *every* experience, particularly those ushered in through what I now believed to be the over-emotionalism of worship. It stopped me cold. I could no longer traverse that road.

Another factor that came into play took a long time to recognize and acknowledge. During times of praise, when I dared for a moment to open my heart, it seemed that God would then begin to probe the wound. In His inimitably kind and patient manner, He was waiting for me to allow Him to search the depths of my heart. No doubt with the intention to administer healing—remove the thorn, apply the disinfectant, bind the wound—but because I was having difficulty with trust, nothing up to that moment seemed a more daunting and thoroughly frightening prospect. He certainly had the prerogative; He is God, and God's dealings with His children always leads to an ultimately favorable end. Yet, I was foolishly clinging to what I considered to be the safer choice. In short, I shut Him out.

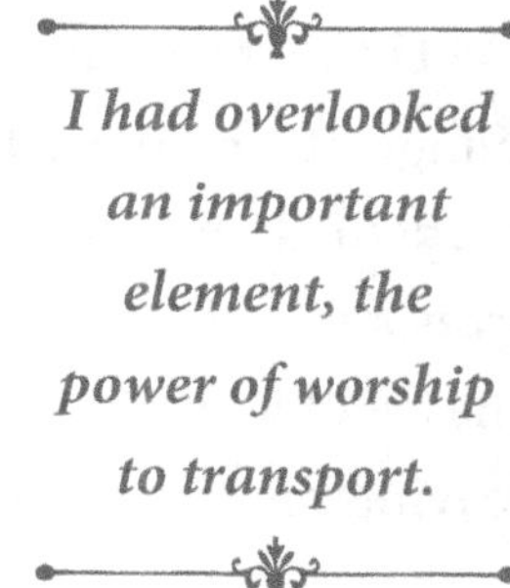

I had overlooked an important element, the power of worship to transport. Through worship, we are enabled to completely forget ourselves. It's our best opportunity to be lifted above circumstances to a place where difficulties are put into their proper perspective. As the lyricist describes:

> *Turn your eyes upon Jesus, look into His wonderful face. And the things of earth will grow strangely dim in the light of his glory and grace.*
>
> —ALAN JACKSON

Ultimately, the Lord had the last word. Motivated by a hunger to connect to Him in a deeper way, after being perpetually wooed by an ongoing demonstration of God's irresistible kindness and love, I finally opened my heart. In the act of worship, the floodgates of joy were again released, leaving me to question why I had ever waited so long.

THE PERIL OF SELF-PITY

"Self-pity is our worst enemy and if we yield to it, we can never do anything wise in this world."

—HELEN KELLER

"Self-pity is a death that has no resurrection, a sinkhole from which no rescuing hand can drag you because you have chosen to sink."

—ELISABETH ELLIOT

If you are newly bereaved, please read this section with caution. Your sorrow in loss is perfectly justified. No thinking person would have the temerity to suggest that your pain is in any way caused by self-pity. It took years—after some of the stings of loss had been eased—for me to realize that it was imperative to my recovery that I address the issue of self-pity, for indeed, a more enervating emotion—other than fear—does not exist. Assenting to that emotion invariably leads to an astonishingly rapid downward slide to depression, which, once initiated, becomes very difficult to reverse.

The term "self-pity" for me instantly conjures an image of Gollum [Sméagol], the bestial character in *The Lord of the Rings Trilogy* and a quintessential embodiment of self-centered self-pity. The image of this slimy character slithering along on his belly—the personification of a dangerously oppressed being—is the very antithesis of its counterpart, an upstanding, faith-speaking, steadfast child of God.

Gollum's idiosyncratic speech: talking to himself in sibilant whispers, his use of illeism—indicative perhaps of a severe identity disorder—and his manner of "hissing and whining," while speaking, represents the twisted expressions of one entirely preoccupied with self. Indeed, the name Gollum, which literally means "a horrible swallowing noise in [the] throat," reminds us of the tight lump in the throat generated by the onset of a wave of self-pity. Gollum's self-indulgence resulted in a grotesque mutation of both body and mind into an unrecognizable form, no doubt attributable to the fact that—in the words of Tolkien—"his head and his eyes were downward."

During times when I was tempted to wallow in self-sorrow, that vivid image would surface as a stern reminder to steer clear. Capitalizing on victimhood is dangerous. Self-pity creates a wide gateway. Unrestrained, it gives us implicit permission to comfort our poor souls with every manner of indulgence. It fuels anger—which, turned inward, is the definition of depression—and sounds the death knell to faith, hope, and joy.

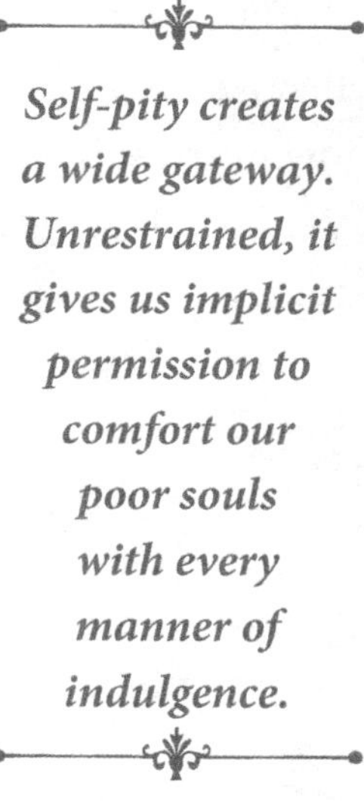

The word "self" is the tip-off; Christians would do well to avoid overfamiliarity with any emotion that feeds the *self* we're instructed to die to. Indeed, we are admonished to be ruthless in eradicating the self-serving tendencies inherent in our human natures. There are very sound reasons for doing so, and they all result in some identifiable good for us. God has provided us with an exhaustive list of benefits that result from reckoning ourselves dead to sin. Our attitudes should reflect all that is wonderful about the salvation and hope we have been generously provided.

Far from being unkind, God's unconventional and effective *Lord of the Rings* analogy rescued me from a dozen downward spirals. Self-pity is, in essence, self-destruction. We allow it, or we disavow it.

A LIFESTYLE OF THANKSGIVING

I cried because I had no shoes, then I met a man who had no feet.

—Mahatma Gandhi

In everything give thanks: for this is the will of God in Christ Jesus concerning you.

—1 Thessalonians 5:18

In times of overwhelming sadness, we must all find ways to cope that are constructive as well as doable. The idea of shouldering one more burden, or task, or responsibility is daunting to individuals who are expending tremendous energy just to "keep it together."

Yet, one of the more important ways I found to help cope with devastating loss is by cultivating an attitude of thankfulness. Those who are in the throes of acute grief might consider this an unfair requirement. It may resemble an impossible task, because it runs counter to everything we may be thinking and feeling. At certain points in our grief journeys, many of us, even those with strong faith, have difficulty seeing any good in our situations. Getting out of bed is tough enough. But being thankful?!

That difficulty is the crux of the matter articulated in Hebrews 13:15. It clearly states that an attitude of thankfulness involves *sacrifice*. It reads:

> *"By Him therefore let us offer the sacrifice of praise to God continually, that is, the fruit of our lips giving thanks to His Name."*

The prophet Habakkuk in vs 3:17-18 offers the same advice even while describing the desolation of having nothing:

> *"Though the fig tree does not bud, and there are no grapes on the vines, though the olive crop fails, and the fields produce no food, though there are no sheep in the pen and no cattle in the stalls, yet I will rejoice in the Lord, I will be joyful in God my Savior."*

How could God be so heartless as to require us to remain thankful no matter what? We may wonder what rationale could possibly exist for a spiritual exercise that seems so counterintuitive. We may question what benefit can be gained from applying this truth.

Arguably the most pertinent rationale is found in Hebrews 13:12:

> *"And so Jesus also suffered outside the city gate to make the people holy through His own blood."*

This verse points to the sacrifice of Jesus as the most significant reason for our continued adoration of Him. His was the ultimate sacrifice. Indeed, where would we be without our Savior, who was so willing to offer Himself without reservation? If nothing else good were ever to happen in our lives again, God sending Jesus to purchase our salvation would be more than sufficient reason for us to thank Him for all eternity.

Added to that, there is even more—much more—to thank God for. Do we have our health? A roof over our heads? Enough to eat? We thank the One who is our provider. Do we still have our wits? Can we get out of bed? Have two working legs and two good arms? We bless the One who sustains us. The list of things to thank God for is endless: our family, a community of caring people, fresh air to breathe, and a beautiful sunset to behold, to name a few. The opportunities to thank God are limited only by our powers of observation and our willingness to appreciate what we have been given.

Beyond the rationale for cultivating thankfulness, there is another factor that comes into play. God graciously answers the question, "What can we possibly gain? The "if-then" of our relationship with God always results in a beneficial outcome for us. Offering thanksgiving turns our focus to the Lord and draws our attention away from ourselves and the pain we live with. Thus redirected, we are less likely to sink to the level of our feelings and more inclined to look outward and, eventually, forward.

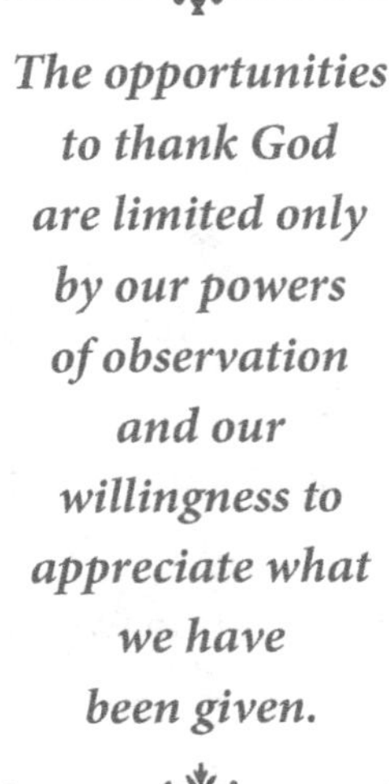
The opportunities to thank God are limited only by our powers of observation and our willingness to appreciate what we have been given.

Finally, the reward of an attitude of thanksgiving is God Himself. He is our "*...exceedingly great reward.*" (Genesis 15:1) Because He "*...inhabits the praises of His people,*" (Psalm 22:3) our God is present with us in our distress. And we know that God's Presence which offers the recipient solace, comfort, guidance, and encouragement—largesse beyond measure compared with our small sacrifice—also ultimately leads to joy:

> *"You will show me the path of life: In your presence is fullness of joy: At your right hand there are pleasures forever."*
>
> **Psalm 16:11**

Yes, maintaining an attitude of praise and thankfulness is uncomfortable. It involves sacrifice. But those who are willing to obey God's Word will ultimately progress from crushing despair to the first fresh glimmers of hope. In this way, we remind ourselves that it's not about us. It will only, ever, and always be about Him.

THE POWER IN HUMOR

"Laugh till you weep. Weep till there's nothing left but to laugh at your weeping. In the end, it's all one."

—FREDERICK BEUCHNER

Then our mouth was filled with laughter, and our tongue with shouts of joy; then they said among the nations, "The Lord has done great things for them."

—PSALMS 126:2

There is a photo of me that I keep at my desk, taken on New Year's Eve at the end of the year 2000. It depicts a youthful, confident woman, smiling joyfully because she finally knew who she was and where she was headed. On one of my bad days, in a fit of pique, I christened it the "last time I was truly happy" picture. Since then, it has served as a reminder of how far I have come in the grief process because that woman's confidence, thought to be forever lost, has finally returned. Better still, her joy has resurfaced, although, to be completely honest, the joy was always there, just a bit obscured. The art of humor played a huge role in uncapping the well of joy. In my experience, humor's usefulness as a healing influence cannot be overstated.

I love to laugh. It is without question an inherited trait. My family enjoys their humor, especially of the satirical variety, and we can always find something to laugh at in just about every situation. Case in point. Mourning is singularly unfunny, and funerals in particular. Yet during my daughter's memorial service, my family kept track of the amusing things that occurred of which I, in my benumbed state, was not aware and, upon returning home, regaled me with story after story.

The art of humor played a huge role in uncapping the well of joy.

They provided details of some of the attendees' hilarious attire, one sporting a hat that resembled Saturn, and reenacted scenes, such as one mourner's dramatic stagger up the aisle to the viewing supported on both sides by her children, her piercing scream upon arriving, prostrating herself over the casket in paroxysms of grief, unquestionably—in my family's view—acting the part of the star performer, with my daughter upstaged into a mere supporting role—the incident made more ridiculous by the fact that the performer had no relationship with my daughter!

My family was doing their best to cheer me up and I was in stitches despite the macabre tone and setting. Of course, the fun didn't last. Still, the uplift it provided was such good medicine that I decided, going forward, to make it a point to regularly seek humor as a counterbalance to sorrow. Laughter also helped me to feel closer to my daughter, whose sparkling sense of humor could always be counted on to lighten any mood.

Humor helped brighten the dreariness of the workplace. I've always been enamored of words, their meanings, etymologies, and derivations. I devour books for breakfast, lunch, and dinner. Therefore, spotting humorous errors in spelling and usage is as natural to me as breathing.

God often used this odd predilection of mine to provide spots of humor to brighten my day.

For example, one of my employers, a mistress of the malaprop to rival the best of Reverend Spooner (he of "Kinquering Congs" fame) [8], became an unintentional stand-up comedian in the process of conducting the weekly staff meeting. My manager and I, seated as far from the front as possible, would turn positively purple with suppressed mirth (God forgive us!) as we listened to this dear hapless woman deliver deadpan a nonstop litany of misused words and non-sequiturs, the supply of which seemed to be deliciously inexhaustible.

For example: we were warned to beware of opening envelopes that contained white powder that could be Amtrak (anthrax); informed of a staff luncheon where stone cold (coal-fired) pizza would be served; and soberly told that the physical (fiscal) year was about to end. We listened in disbelief as the groundskeepers were instructed

---

[8] Reverend Spooner was an Anglican clergyman whose malaprops in the form of word transpositions were so memorable they became known as "Spoonerisms."

to thrash (thatch) the lawn (as punishment for producing those patches of brown?); and hopelessly convulsed when the secretary was ordered to write a memo regarding the smell *emancipating* from the men's room (all the phews that's fit to print?). We barely survived these sessions with our dignity intact, but it got some of us through the otherwise insufferably dull week.

Students' essays provided another much-anticipated source of fresh comedic fodder. As a language arts teacher, spotting mangled language was my mission and specialty. One essayist wrote about a raper (rapper) they admired, another described the thrill of jumping out of an airplane with a pair of shoes (parachute), and many routinely mangled idiomatic expressions, such as two peas in a pot (pod) and it's a doggie-dog world, (dog eat dog), to my endless amusement. My all-time favorite? "Your (You're) the best language arts teacher ever!" (*Is that so?)* I was always looking for any excuse to have a laugh, never mind that it was at someone else's, anyone else's, or my own expense!

The silly antics of my students were also a wonderful source of joy. I began my teaching career in a moldy, comically decrepit portable classroom located a good distance from the main building. One torrential rainstorm set the stage for the best belly laugh of the year. Class had already begun when a conga line of latecomers, pushing and shoving in their haste to get in out of the rain, slipped on the cracked, wet threshold and fell down like a row of dominoes. No one was hurt but watching my classroom floor turn into an impromptu slip-and-slide left me weak-kneed with hilarity. You may judge me as an irresponsible teacher. But whom, might I ask, is immune to slapstick?

Holidays were my least favorite times of the year, so employing humor helped me to make the best of a bad season. On one occasion, while I was (mis)handling sparklers, the straw on my espadrilles caught fire, causing me to commence a maniacal flamenco on the lawn to extinguish the flames, much to the intense amusement of the onlookers. My nephews, convulsed with laughter after surveying the charred heels of my unfortunate shoes, rolled on the ground clutching their stomachs.

During yet another Fourth of July fiasco, my sister became an unwitting hostess to a wildly explosive party. While exiting through the front door—I was just in time to hear a single panicked drawn-out word "Rrruuuuunnn!" — and witness an errant bomb, streaking down as a bolt from heaven, exploding the food table, sending flutes and canapés airborne, and spurting fire and sparks that chased startled guests out of their chairs and down the street. I looked up to see the ashen face of my brother-in-law who, in an attempt to create a dramatic and memorable fireworks tour de force, had accidentally dropped a lit massive mortar from the second-floor railing. Fortunately, no one was injured, but I do not recall ever laughing so hard and so long.

Life is filled with funny moments. If we fail to see them or decide not to seek them, we may lose the best opportunity to forget ourselves.

NATURE AS HEALER

'The heavens declare the glory of God; and the firmament shows his handiwork.

—PSALM 19:1

"Oh, these vast, calm, measureless mountain days, days in whose light everything seems equally divine, opening a thousand windows to show us God."

—JOHN MUIR

I never appreciated the value of spending time in nature until it became an absolute must. Endless hours spent indoors—beginning with a long commute and then shut up all day within the four walls of a classroom enduring the same sights, same sounds, same *smells*—nearly smothered the life out of me.

I craved the outdoors. Jogging late at night afforded a welcome, albeit temporary, release. During those hours, there was—thankfully—no one to talk to and fewer cars to contend with. The hushed, deep stillness of night often moved me to tears. Reluctant to go back inside, I dragged my mattress onto the screened porch of my top-floor apartment and slept where I could gaze upon the stars that glittered like cut crystal and feel the soft night breezes on my face. I would have gladly camped there permanently.

My intense fascination with nature began one day at the beach. Sitting on a towel gazing at the sea, I reached over to scoop up a handful of sand. I was awestruck to discover that it was comprised of many, perhaps dozens of, perfectly formed miniature white seashells. Staring at these tiny marvels, I experienced a moment of complete and unalloyed delight.

The shells delivered an important message; their uniformity of color and perfection of symmetry underscored the absolute unlikelihood, the sheer impossibility, of their existing by mere chance. They could never in a million years have happened without design. This represented a turning point for me. To acknowledge that chance was not a factor that I had to reckon with was a deeply reassuring concept for someone who so keenly felt the apparent randomness of one life-changing accident. God, relentless seeker of lost sheep, had through nature provided a door of communication with me.

Months later, God again delivered a meaningful message through nature. While I was walking through the woods, a leaf floated down from above and landed softly on my shoulder. Examining it closely, I discovered a beautifully constructed delicately veined work of art, resplendent in the gorgeously riotous hues of fall. Each color looked as if it had been hand-painted; burnished orange subtlety feather-brushed into the crimson, stem tinged with still fresh vibrant green, and leaf edges gilded gold. The fact that God would take such pains to make an ephemeral object so magnificent spoke volumes to me of His unquestioned care for all of His creations, including me. Such objects, created for His pleasure and for ours, demonstrate His purposeful intention to make all things beautiful.

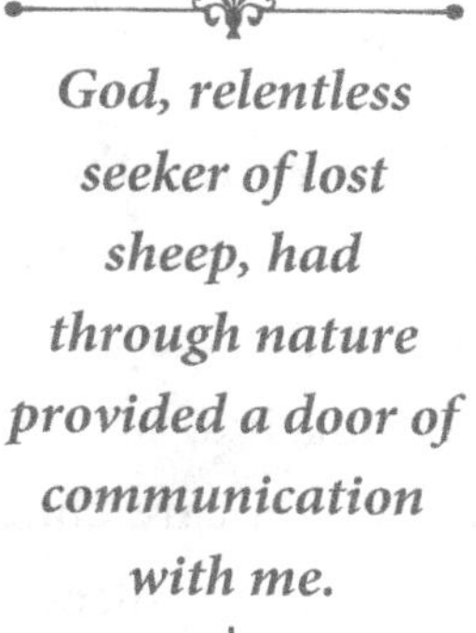
God, relentless seeker of lost sheep, had through nature provided a door of communication with me.

Time spent in nature became time spent with God. I couldn't seem to get high enough. Hiking the beautiful San Gabriel Mountains, scaling Sandia Peak, and climbing the rock-hewn steps of Yosemite's Vernal Falls, in the similitude of a pilgrimage, brought me ever closer to heaven. I would shout exuberant greetings to my daughter and my God from the summits. All life's vicissitudes—troubles and grief among them—were summarily dwarfed and given perspective from these eagle's nest vantage points.

Breathing the woodsy rarified atmosphere of hyper-oxygenated air and the heady fragrance of pine—taking it in by the gulps—I sensed life, the very breath of God, seeping into all the weary places, and releasing the tight bundle of care clutched around my heart. And oh, how I savored the silence—a deep abiding silence that slowly, finally, quieted the inner chaos of my soul.

The message gleaned from nature is a clarion call that awakens us to the order and sense of an infinitely wise and preeminent Creator. Nature, as a reflection of a loving God, is enduring, consistently available, and easily accessed—a precious resource that, to this day, moves me to the core.

IN THE MASTER'S SERVICE

"...You are not your own; you were bought at a price. Therefore, honor God with your bodies."

— 1 CORINTHIANS 6:19-20 NIV

"...whoever desires to become great among you, let him be your servant.

— MATTHEW 20:26

The greatest and most powerful human being ever to grace the earth lived an example so out of the ordinary it was undefinable by any recognizable standard. He seemed the antithesis of most mortal concepts of a "successful" person. Yet, in three short years of public ministry, He managed to turn the world so completely upside-down it has never been the same. This He accomplished with little fanfare and zero self-aggrandizement.

Wearing humility as a garment, this God-Man served His fellow man tirelessly, patiently, and from a heart filled with love and compassion. To know Him was to love Him, as many of his disciples would attest. Knowing Him changed them profoundly. In like manner, when we as believers experience God's high level of love, we also are forever changed. Those who are wise follow Him anywhere and strive to imitate the lover of their souls.

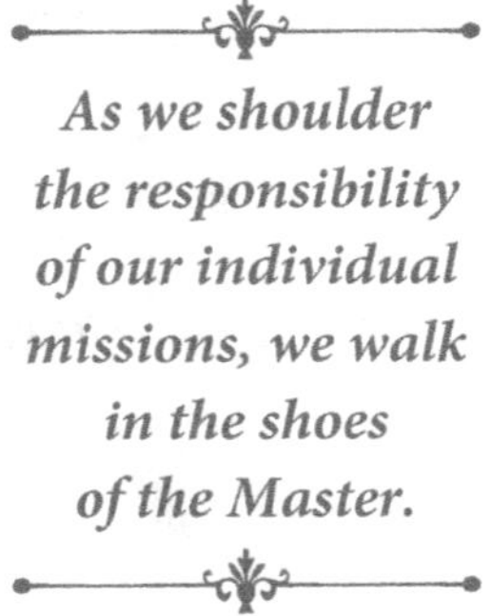
As we shoulder the responsibility of our individual missions, we walk in the shoes of the Master.

For Jesus indeed modeled for us the path to an authentic life, one in which our greatest fulfillment comes through service to mankind. As we shoulder the responsibility of our individual missions, we walk in the shoes of the Master. It becomes our privilege and great honor to serve Him, and this service in turn becomes the magnum opus of our lives here on earth.

While in His service, astonishing things begin to happen both within us and around us. We experience wisdom beyond our intellect, strength beyond our natural means, and seasons of incomprehensible courage.

Recognizing that His strength is perfected in our weakness, we learn to lean heavily upon the Lord each day with the result that the good outcomes become *His* rather than ours. We find safety, as well as great joy, resting in His everlasting arms.

It is not easy to persevere when misfortune comes our way. It can also be challenging to rouse ourselves to tasks when we would prefer sheltering in our comfort zones. In both cases, we can rest assured that as we continue to obey our instructions, we will somehow find the strength to carry them out.

The greatest healing occurs when we make a deliberate effort to forget ourselves and find others to bless. It is the best—and often only—panacea for our pain.

THE ROLE OF TIME

> *"Willpower does not change men. Time does not change men. Christ does."*
>
> —Henry Drummond

Shortly after Lisa's passing, I attended a few meetings sponsored by a local chapter of The Compassionate Friends, an organization created to provide support to bereaved parents. The couple who led the sessions had lost their little girl to a drunk driver ten years before. In view of their loss, I found their equanimity to be nothing less than amazing, for in those first months of agonizing grief, I could not imagine ever feeling normal again.

Their attitude gave me hope that one day I too could come back from this horror to a life that bore some resemblance to sanity and stability. Their example was meaningful due to our shared experience as well as those of others in attendance—some were veterans of many more years of loss—who, against all odds, had learned to cope in constructive and deeply meaningful ways.

It has been said that time heals all wounds. That adage does not necessarily hold true, for time can be the greatest foe to those who are wounded. A long stretch of time, rather than serving as an agent of healing, can instead exacerbate a festering wound. An ongoing attitude of anger or unforgiveness for example, carefully cultivated year after year, can devolve into a lifetime of bitterness. In the case of the bereaved, the passage of time often marks endless years suffused with missed milestones and unabated loneliness. Time alone cannot be assigned the task of healing; it is not sufficient for the challenge.

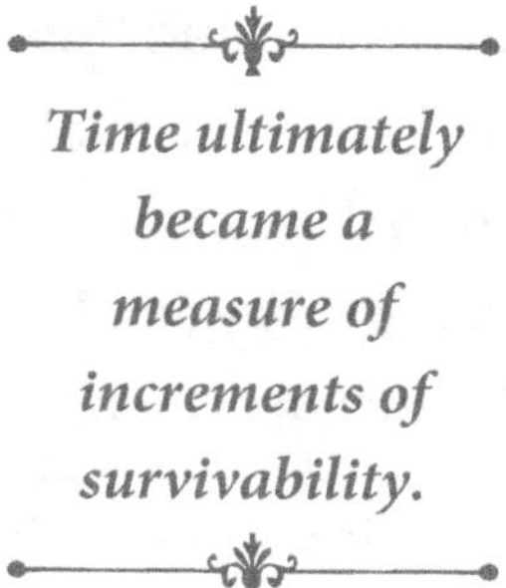

The more authentic use of time in the life of the bereaved Christian occurs when we open our hearts and allow God ample room to fill our days with Him. In my experience, leaning heavily upon Him when the going got rough—in essence, toughing it out—when it seemed that all was lost, was only achievable to the degree that I learned to exchange strengths.

During times of intense grief, I would dash to my prayer closet like Clark Kent to a phone booth seeking a spiritual change of clothing. There, I would implore God to enrobe me with *His* strength and carry me through the impossible moments, and thus in effect, "put on Christ," as instructed in Romans 13:14. Even in my state of relative estrangement from Him, the Lord never once failed in those times to come to my aid. Invariably, I was able to keep going garbed in the Superman vestments of His strength.

Time ultimately became a measure of increments of survivability. As each day dawned, I was faced with the choice to either embrace the day or just endure it. Early in the process, it seemed I had no option but to choose the latter. But as years went by, the pain began to ease, aided by distance from the event, an enhanced ability to cope, and an awareness of the bright possibilities inherent in each day. I reasoned that since I had come this far, God would surely see me through to the end.

Indeed, each day I live carries me ever closer to an eventual reunion with my precious Savior and my beautiful daughter. The anticipation of that blissful event propels me forward with joy.

A "REINVESTMENT" CHRONICLE

"I've read the last page of the Bible. It's all going to turn out all right."

—BILLY GRAHAM

"Leave the broken, irreversible past in God's hands, and step out into the invincible future with Him."

—OSWALD CHAMBERS

"For I know the plans I have for you," declares the Lord, "plans to prosper you and not to harm you, plans to give you hope and a future."

—JEREMIAH 29:11

In my first book, I expressed great admiration for bereaved parents who had worked through their grief by reinvesting their lives into the lives of others. I dared to hope that in time I too could be used by God to positively impact those around me. I could not have anticipated how the path would unfold or foresee the many twists and turns that would ensue in the pursuit of that purpose.

When Lisa died, I had just completed my undergraduate degree. Returning to school in my forties, having separated from my husband and a marriage of more than twenty years seemed at the time to be the most difficult feat imaginable. How little I understood what truly defined a difficulty! I had just secured full-time employment at a university library. It was a starting place that I was thankful for, but it did not last long. I resigned when I just couldn't face being there, in that town, in that apartment, after what occurred.

The disability checks soon ran out, and I had no other source of income. I moved in temporarily with a friend, then with family, thus beginning a long stretch of displacement that encompassed fourteen years. Every one of those years, however, marked a gradual ascent to stability and, ultimately, healing. First came employment in a public relations position with a dependable salary and benefits, then a real estate license, and then a mortgage broker's license.

In perpetual survival mode, I worked all three industries simultaneously, often putting in twelve-hour days. Work had become my sole method of coping. Those workaholic years ultimately paid off—stable employment and careful budgeting eventually led to a home purchase and the end of my life as a nomad—but the punishing work schedule took an enormous physical and emotional toll. Still, with God's help, I persevered.

After several years of creating faux news and planning large events under stressful deadlines, I'd had enough of PR. Feeling as if I still had plenty of the mothering instinct—and needing to be needed—I sought purpose through teaching in a Title I school. This move necessitated yet more schooling in order to qualify for a teaching certificate and eventually resulted in my obtaining a Masters in education.

In all those years, it happened that what I really sought never actually materialized. Purpose, in the form of a life's work, continually eluded me, and as much as I thought I might find—when scanning my students' adorable faces—another pair of eyes that matched my daughter's, it was never to be. What I instead discovered was a composite of her from among them, and I fell head over heels in love with them all. I enjoyed my students immensely and for a good long while was richly sustained through the act of pouring into their young lives.

Teaching presented its own unique set of challenges, a fact that any veteran teacher will attest to. Those challenges, coupled with the almost daily trauma of watching my students interact with their parents and going on with their lives as usual, I marvel now how I, still in the early stages of grief, was able to endure it. The first several years, I wept nearly every day on my drive there and the drive home. Walking the halls and classrooms with a smile plastered on my face was pure performance—a flawless impersonation of a tragi-comic Pagliacci. Being so busy gave me precious little time to think, and that helped me to keep the grief (mostly) at bay. Even in that fiction, God was nigh.

Many days I felt sure I was redefining exhaustion. The student body represented a myriad of complicated discipline problems, the system was unbelievably flawed and antiquated, and the curriculum so sketchy and inflexible that I had to re-create and supplement like mad. Mandatory participation in professional development classes during the year and in the summer, countless hours preparing lessons, marking papers, and gathering classroom materials—all while continuing to sell real estate—virtually ensured that not a single hour would be spent in idleness. Endless duties resulted in uninterrupted isolation, for indeed, there was no time left to develop any semblance of a social life.

Far from a sycophant, it wasn't long before I became gradually disaffected with the profession, largely due to forced participation in peripherals that had absolutely nothing to do with teaching. I was brought to a point of weary exasperation from feigning interest at faculty and staff meetings—both which induced a nearly insufferable and stultifying boredom—and frustrated by the "kill and drill" instruction engendered by high stakes testing.

Isolation, restlessness, and disillusionment dovetailed to create a severe crisis point. Thoughts of failure assailed me, and fears for the future haunted my days. I was nearing 60! How could I keep going amidst utter discouragement and outright exhaustion? I questioned whether this burnout was the result of year after year subsisting as the proverbial square peg in a round hole, for indeed I knew from the outset that teaching children was not my calling.

Grief is an odd fellow; those who grieve often find themselves believing in their own singularity. I struggled not to be defined by that experience. Instinctively I also knew not to park on the "I will nevers." To adopt the attitude of half-empty would be suicide and invariably sound the death knell to forward motion. Indeed, scripture commands the Christian to "gird up the loins of your (our) mind(s)" (1 Peter 1:13), thus making crystal clear the part we play in our own recovery.

Yet had I not done this time and again? At this juncture, I was forced to admit that I had soldiered on as far as I could alone. I had tried everything within me to remain strong, to think positively, and to never give in, and I was failing. The battle for the mind thus began in earnest leaving me, in its wake, feeling as helpless as a child.

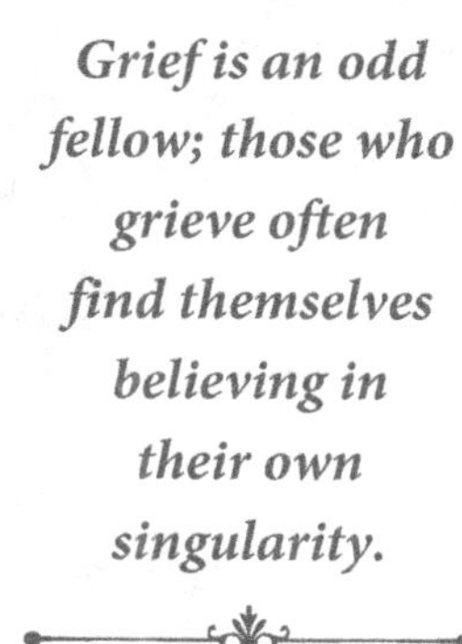

Upon reflection, I realized that I was completely skeptical regarding the promises of God as represented in scripture. God's promises for provision, restoration, love, and mercy, seemed to have utterly eluded me. Had God abandoned me? Or, in acting as my *own* God and deciding my *own* fate, had I actually abandoned Him? Nothing seemed to remain of the former passion and fire I once had for God and for Christian service. Prayer seemed ineffectual. There existed a vacuum in my soul, a "dead space" that seemed unfillable.

This low point was the catalyst to complete surrender. With every other *try* utterly exhausted, I realized that to continue on the same path would be living the definition of insanity. Despite all my efforts, I found I could not mend my broken heart, nor find God's path for my life. A scripture from Matthew (10:39) playing over and over in my mind pointed the way out. Jesus said:

> *"To save your life is to lose it, and to lose your life for my sake is to save it."*

Maintaining the pretense of being in control was exhausting. I knew it would be foolhardy not to allow God to take over.

Thus, I arrived at the day when I finally relinquished to God (again) the absolute and complete control over my life. The decision to surrender made in blind faith became, in the passage of time, the first step to renewal. In searching for a different experience, I understood the wisdom in simply allowing my life to unfold. I was finally at peace. And, who knew, perhaps someone, somewhere, held the missing piece to the puzzle of purpose.

Soon after, along came the man who would become my second husband. I had never been in a relationship in the years since my separation and divorce. For some reason, during what I termed the summer of my discontent, I decided to begin dating, which I did occasionally sharing coffee and conversation when I could find the time. Yet, unerringly, almost from the moment a gentleman and I were seated across from one another, I would hear an inward voice say, "He's not *the one*." Those fellows became the unwitting victims of the one-date-wonder woman.

I had just about given up on the whole process, when I met Jim. On our first coffee date, I waited to hear the predictable inner voice. This time, however, the voice was strangely silent. Intrigued, I agreed to a second date. When the food arrived, my date bowed his head and gave thanks for the meal. I was impressed. As we became better acquainted, I found him to be a wonderful man of God who was unfailingly kind, patient, and understanding. He was just what I needed at just the right time. We were married in 2015.

He has two daughters from his first marriage, women who love God. They are not replacements for Lisa but two wonderful additions to my life. They continue to enrich and broaden my worldview. I love them dearly for the joy that they bring.

My husband has taken me on many inspirational journeys to the national parks, provided me with a lovely extended family, and offered unfailing support in my dreams and aspirations. It was upon his suggestion that I decided to retire from teaching to devote more time to writing.

In addition, my husband and I head a non-profit organization that assists the bereaved. We provide resources and encouragement to individuals and families who have suffered profound loss. The work is immensely gratifying.

Where God will lead from here remains to be seen. In articulating these musings, the full progression from disbelief to unbelief, then back to belief, stands out in bas-relief. God never changes, and one incontrovertible truth of the matter remains; we are the ones who are in need of change. In due time and in His own way, He changed me.

CHAPTER 4

FINDING GOD: YOUR STORY

WHAT IS "THE SINNER'S PRAYER?"

The "sinner's prayer" designates a prayer that is used to express one's desire to have a personal relationship with God through Jesus Christ. In this act, an individual is acknowledging that they are subject to errors, mistakes, and sins and are in a fallen state of separation from God. The prayer further expresses an individual's *repentance* from past ways, a term that means simply to turn and go in the opposite direction.

Finally, the prayer expresses the belief that Jesus Christ was sent by God as our substitute to suffer the punishment for sin in our place. Through His death and resurrection, Jesus satisfied all the claims of justice, thus reconciling sinful man to a holy God, whose provision is for all who simply receive it. The prayer evidences a decision, it only needs to be prayed once, and indicates the outward expression of an individual's heart.

The scriptural references for this experience include the following:

John 1:12,

"But as many as received Him (Jesus), to them He gave the power to become the sons of God, [even] to them as believe on His Name."

Romans 10:9-10,

"...that if you confess with your mouth Jesus as Lord and believe in your heart that God raised Him from the dead, you shall be saved; 10 for with the heart man believes, resulting in righteousness, and with the mouth he confesses, resulting in salvation."

Acts 16:30,

"...and after he brought them out, he said, ***"Sirs, what must I do to be saved?" 31 And they said, "Believe in the Lord Jesus, and you shall be saved, you and your household."***

Of course, reciting the prayer or simply saying the words absent any heartfelt sincerity or understanding of our true state before a sinless God, will be nothing more than an empty spiritual exercise.

J.D. Greerer explains it thus:

> *"It's not the prayer that saves; it's the repentance and faith behind the prayer that leads to salvation."*

Our God who sees into every heart can distinguish our intent.

One beautiful prayer of repentance from the Old Testament is the prayer of King David found in Psalms 51.

> *"Have mercy on me, O God, according to Your unfailing love; according to Your great compassion blot out my transgressions. Wash away all my iniquity and cleanse me from my sin. For I know my transgressions, and my sin is always before me. Against You, You only, have I sinned and done what is evil in Your sight, so that You are proved right when You speak and justified when You judge. Surely, I have been a sinner from birth, sinful from the time my mother conceived me . . . . Cleanse me*

> *with hyssop, and I will be clean; wash me and I will be whiter than snow . . . . Create in me a pure heart, O God, and renew a steadfast spirit within me. Do not cast me from Your presence or take Your Holy Spirit from me. Restore to me the joy of Your salvation and grant me a willing spirit to sustain me. Then will I teach transgressors Your ways, and sinners will turn back to You.*

Another very early example of the Sinner's Prayer can be found in Chapter 18 of the *Pilgrim's Progress* written by John Bunyan in 1678.

> *"God be merciful to me a sinner and make me to know and believe in Jesus Christ; for I see, that if his righteousness had not been, or I have not faith in that righteousness, I am utterly cast away. Lord, I have heard that thou art a merciful God, and hast ordained that thy Son Jesus Christ should be the Savior of the world; and moreover, that thou art willing to bestow him upon such a poor sinner as I am-and I am a sinner indeed. Lord, take therefore this opportunity, and magnify thy grace in the salvation of my soul, through thy Son Jesus Christ. Amen."*

So how do you pray the prayer? Although there is no official prayer, the following are several suggested prayers provided as examples. They offer glimpses into a sincere seeker's heart and mind. When you wish to pray, simply choose the one with which you feel most comfortable and pray it from your heart.

***

"Heavenly Father, I realize I am a sinner separated from you. I can never reach heaven by my own good deeds. But you have made provision for my sin. Right now I place my faith in Jesus Christ as God's Son who died for my sins and rose from the dead to give me eternal life. Please forgive me for my sins and help me to live for you. Thank you for accepting me and giving me eternal life." Amen

***

Dear Lord, I admit that I am a sinner. I have done many things that don't please you. I have lived my life for myself only. I am sorry, and I repent. I ask you to forgive me.

Jesus, I believe that you died on the cross for me, to save me. You did what I could not do for myself. I come to you now and ask you to take control of my life; I give it to you. From this day forward, help me to live every day for you and in a way that pleases you. I love you, Lord, and I thank you that I will spend all eternity with you. Amen.

***

Dear Father in heaven, I come to you in the name of Jesus. I acknowledge to You that I am a sinner, and I am sorry for my sins and the life that I have lived; I need your forgiveness. I believe that your Son Jesus Christ shed His precious blood on the cross at Calvary and died for my sins, and I am now willing to turn from my sin.

You said in Your holy Word, Romans 10:9, that if we confess the Lord our God and believe in our hearts that God raised Jesus from the dead, we shall be saved. Right now, I confess Jesus as the Lord of my soul. With my heart, I believe that God raised Jesus from the dead. This very moment I accept Jesus Christ as my Savior, and according to His Word, right now I am saved.

Thank you, Jesus, for your unlimited grace, which has saved me from my sins. Therefore, Lord Jesus, transform my life so that I may bring glory and honor to you alone and not to myself. Thank you, Jesus, for dying for me and giving me eternal life. Amen.

After you pray that prayer, tell someone. Confess it publicly.

FOR THE SKEPTIC

"Everyone who calls on the name of the Lord will be saved."

—ROMANS 10:13

That you have read this far is heartening. Yet so many questions remain. You may wonder why mankind requires "salvation" of the type outlined in scriptures and espoused by Christians. As a young seeker of truth, I remember pursuing the same line of questioning and feeling slightly offended by the use of the term "saved," and the phrase "being born again." I wondered what the human race was allegedly being saved from and born again to. Although the words "born again" (found in John, Chapter 3 and originally articulated by Christ) forms the cornerstone of the Christian faith, I did not understand its importance any more than I could comprehend the issue of salvation. The desire for answers eventuated in a lengthy journey toward the truth. What I discovered rather shocked me.

During my middle school years our family relocated to a new community. This move became the catalyst that accelerated my intense search for spiritual meaning. Our family began to attend services at a local Methodist church where a charismatic and eloquent pastor held the pulpit. There, I joined a youth group, and there also I was first introduced to the concept of what is referred to as "original sin." A sensitive, naïve, and comparatively sheltered seventh grader experiencing what could be described as a fairly idyllic childhood, I found it rather worrisome to be the recipient of sermon after sermon on the evils of sin.

More odd was the profound effect those admonitions had on me, for I took them to heart and wondered gravely whether sin was something I needed to pay closer attention to, no pun intended. After all, the congregation had been recently reminded that they were all sinners, and although it was a tremendous relief not to be singled out as the only errant sheep, the concept of being something other than good was deeply disturbing to me. I once ventured to ask my mother if she thought I was a good person and her predictably favorable answer, "*Of course you are,*" did little to assuage my fear. I rationalized that a mother who was not God would naturally endorse a less exacting standard of behavior, especially in view of the fact that most of my childish transgressions—the more egregious ones in particular—were committed entirely without her knowledge.

To illustrate the Christian perspective from a theological standpoint, the concept of original sin describes humanity's fallen state that purportedly resulted from Adam and Eve's rebellion in the Garden of Eden. Momentarily placing to one side our views on whether the account should be viewed as fantastical, literal, or allegorical, the sequence of events—temptation, decision, consequence—is undeniably reenacted daily in the multitude of moments that comprise the human condition.

As iterated in the book of Genesis, God provided the couple everything they could possibly wish to eat and drink yet forbade them from eating from a particular tree, the tree of the knowledge of good and evil. He warned that their disobedience to His directive would result in their deaths. According to the account, a serpent, considered the reptilian embodiment of Satan, tempted the woman to eat from the tree. Interestingly, in the Genesis account, Adam was standing alongside the woman and fully participating in the transgression—this mention categorically challenging all the misogynist nonsense of woman as eternal malefactor, for although she was deceived, he apparently was not.

When they partook of the tree in defiance of a direct order from God—based on a decision that demonstrated a deplorable breech of loyalty—the result was the permanent rearrangement of their relationship with God, which before had been close and companionable. Much like betrayal in a marriage, the couple made the decision to change their allegiance and what was done could not be undone. Though spared an immediate death—Adam and Eve *did* face physical death as an eventuality—they, in effect, more inexorably perished in the spiritual death that ensued. This spiritual death, considered to be the ultimate separation from God, manifested consequences both temporal and eternal. The act of rebellion, however, was emblematic of much more.

What actually occurred in this momentous event in the Garden, this "fall of man," was the inception in mankind of a *nature* or tendency to wrongdoing that was at cross-purposes to God's design. To understand this fully necessitates an individual believing in the existence of evil and also its occurrence through human agency as the rule rather than the exception. There are many who do not agree that evil exists within, who view mankind as essentially good—that children, in particular, are innately good—and that the tendency to wrongdoing is nothing more than learned behavior.

That evil exists in the world should be evident. One need only consult any news source in any city on any given day to understand that moment-by-moment, evil choices are made over good ones. That a tendency to self-will is instinctive can be demonstrated by simply asking toddlers to divest themselves of any object they consider *theirs*—and witness the result. Visit any school and observe the heartbreaking cruelty that children routinely exhibit towards one another.

Our certainty of the existence of evil rests more on whether we believe that evil exists within *us*. An honest assessment of one's own inner thoughts and feelings, especially when challenged—particularly unfairly—clearly points to a tendency to think negatively of the perpetrator.

We point to the standards of fairness, never questioning from where they stem, or from whom, and inevitably rise to our own defense.

Although we may anger easily, or imbibe to excess, or experience the gamut of harmful emotions, we magnanimously excuse ourselves, focusing instead on the collective of others' evils. We remain unperturbed by our own wrong thinking and wrongdoing. A clear-sighted assessment of human nature, or even a cursory glimpse into one's own heart and actions, should suffice to make the case that we are not essentially good.

Contrary to what we may think, God's issue is not with sinful man or, as we've been led to assume, with an individual's sins, but rather with a particular *nature*. Illustrating the Christian perspective found in New Testament scripture, God's wrath is against a *nature*, not the person.

Indeed, when Christ confronted members of the religious order of the day, he stated the fact that they were of their father, the devil (John 8:44). The Messiah was not indulging in puerile and pettish name-calling but rather, from the superior perspective of the omnipotent, stating the fact that all those born from Adam are born with this adverse *nature*. God knows we are powerless to change our natures. He is not angry with us, individually or collectively, for missing the mark. His anger is against a nature. Ephesians 2:3-4 states that individuals "...were by *nature* the children of wrath. But God who is rich in mercy...made us alive together in Christ."

How unfairly then, one might argue, is this hideous burden of sin nature foisted upon us! How could a single traitorous act become the sole cause of having sin nature visited upon every living soul from time immemorial? Where is the justice in that? Should the child be judged by the sins of the father? Is mankind a pawn in some cataclysmic power struggle between two opposing forces? At first glance, it would seem so. However, to place the entire panorama of human suffering at the feet of God is to do Him an unspeakable injustice. In our censure, we fail to factor in the one essential element material to our own rescue, the element of choice.

Human suffering is not God's punishment, nor His design. We may cite Old Testament examples at will, yet there is nevertheless within them a clear differentiation between the permissive and the causative will. Ample warning not to violate either spiritual or natural law was always offered to avert catastrophe—leap off a building, you fall to the ground. Yet consistently, mankind's choice has been to ignore God's admonitions and go his own way. God could, at any moment, arbitrarily interfere with mankind's choices or nullify mankind's freedom to choose altogether. He does neither.

When Christ as Savior was sent into the world, His prime directive was to undo the damage wrought by Adam's rebellion. The purpose was to free mankind from the enslavement to a nature that imprisons us, and dooms us, into harmful patterns of behavior. This was accomplished through Christ's death in a substitutionary role. A righteous God could justifiably punish mankind for our aggregate sin. And lest we question the need for justice, think how little respect we would grant law enforcement or the courts if they failed to render justice due! Instead of punishing mankind to satisfy the claims of justice, God instead laid the sin of mankind on the willing shoulders of His Son. Suffice to say, the provision was made, and the price was paid.

When we decide to receive Christ's sacrifice for us—and pledge our allegiance to Him as God's representative—an exchange of *natures* takes place in us. This change is articulated in the words of the apostle Paul: "Therefore if any man be in Christ, he is *a new creation*; old things are passed away, behold all things become new." (2 Corinthians 5:17). God essentially removes our old nature and replaces it with His. (2 Peter 1:4) This mystery of redemption creates a new order of existence. A brand new person comes into being, one who is "born again." This is indeed the sum of the Good News.

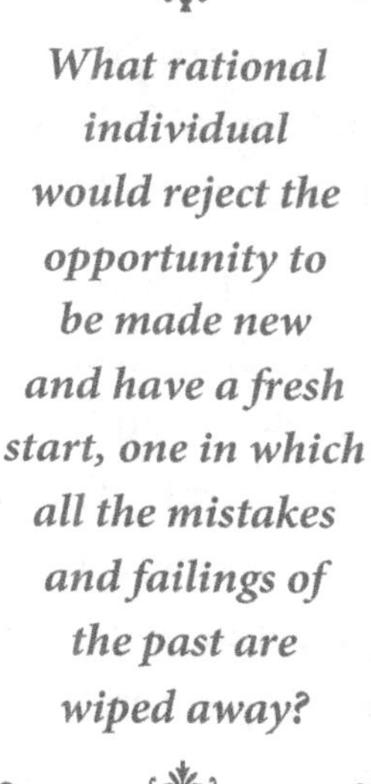
What rational individual would reject the opportunity to be made new and have a fresh start, one in which all the mistakes and failings of the past are wiped away?

What person possessed of their faculties, would not welcome a second chance at life? What rational individual would reject the opportunity to be made new and have a fresh start, one in which all the mistakes and failings of the past are wiped away? More to the point, given the choice to communicate with a loving God—who unquestionably possesses the most marvelous and scintillating intellect in the universe, who answers your questions, dries your tears, and provides direction for the rest of your life—why would anyone refuse?

Yet in all cases, mankind is given the choice to accept or reject this provision. Our many attempts to fix ourselves, to live right, to think correctly, to do good works—in short, to circumvent God's provision for establishing our righteousness (literally, *right standing*) with Him and substitute it with our own—are just more of the same, myriad examples of humankind's ongoing self-will and rebellion. We alone cast the deciding vote: to accept God's gift or reject it. The choice is— and has always been — irrevocably ours.

AFTERWORD

ON THE DEPARTED

The photo on the back cover of this book was taken from a hot air balloon flying over the city of Albuquerque at 9,000 feet above sea level. Though idyllic in appearance the picture belies reality for, at that moment, the passengers in that balloon—of which I was one—were in danger. Our balloon had gotten stuck— stranded in the doldrums, the essential breeze for navigation having completely ceased—and we remained aloft for quite some time, with no apparent movement in any direction. We were far from our launch site with no safe place to land.

The journey had begun as a glorious front-row seat to a breathtaking sunrise. Gaining altitude, we'd glided over terrain of the lushest green interspersed with stretches of mocha-hued lunar desert. We had crossed the Rio Grande, silvered mercurial with the dawn's white light, and flown near mountains shrouded in lowering purple mist. Climbing higher, much higher than nearby balloons, we'd beheld a city in miniature, dwarfed by distance, still in slumber. Almost miraculously, a rainbow had materialized, appearing to follow us everywhere. It was a stunningly beautiful, picture-perfect day.

And then…it wasn't.

Floating in the fragile wicker gondola, our lives literally hanging in the balance, we overheard the pilot on his cellphone calmly requesting permission for an emergency landing on the reservation. As we waited, the day grew uncomfortably warm. The other passengers—two couples and a mother and daughter—were struggling to remain calm, laughing nervously at nothing, making small talk. Eventually, all fell silent. Needless to say, the situation afforded each passenger a sterling opportunity for reflection.

I wondered then whether I would die that day. It didn't really matter much to me, but I was worried for the others. Were *they* ready to die? Did they know God? What would be their eternal destinies?

***

Many have pondered the reality of heaven and hell and the finality they represent. These subjects engender an endless list of questions. Does heaven exist? Does hell? What about those who have died not knowing Christ? How can someone who has never heard the gospel be sent to hell?

If a person has led a less than holy life, can they make it to heaven, even at the last minute? What about people who believe in other religions? Yet among the myriad questions, one alone is the most pertinent to those who have lost someone: *"Is my loved one in heaven?"*

The advent of sophisticated methods of resuscitation and rescue has led to a proliferation of books describing near-death experiences. Nearly all point to the existence of a hereafter. Some describe heaven-like surroundings, while others' depictions are frighteningly hellish.

Amid the cacophony, one intriguing account detailing the phenomenon of "life flashing before our eyes" is worth noting. The story describes one minister's near-death experience when the aircraft he was traveling in crash-landed. According to his account, their small plane had begun to lose altitude almost from the moment of takeoff and belly-flopped to earth quickly and violently. Although terribly injured, both he and the pilot survived. The time they knew a crash was imminent to the moment they hit the ground was about 4 seconds.

What occurred during those four seconds was truly remarkable. In that brief space of time, the minister's life passed through his consciousness in vivid panorama. Every memorable incident both good and bad—from scenes as a toddler being impudent to his mother, through the sins of his youth, to his conversion experience, his marriage, the birth of his children, and highlights of his ministry—flashed by in milliseconds.

A sheer impossibility, one might think, both psychologically and physiologically. And yet somehow, it happened. The point, driven dramatically home in those few breathless seconds, was a lesson of importance. Even at the last moment, when death seemed inevitable, this man knew that he was being offered a window of choice. As a Christian, he was, of course, immensely relieved to remember that he had long ago made that choice.

The enormous significance of this account is the recognition that those near death may very well be afforded a similar window of opportunity to choose God. It would be a very hardened person indeed who, upon seeing their entire life pass before them in stark review, would decide not to call upon the name of the Lord. More astonishingly, it appears that those thus imperiled who cry to God in true penitence, even at the last second, are granted mercy.

We have scriptural proof of the "last-minute mercy" of God when we recall the story of the penitent thief found in Luke 23:39-43. Christ was crucified between two thieves, both who viciously mocked and reviled Him. One of them, finally coming to his senses, acknowledged his life of crime and, in an act of true repentance, asked to be remembered when Christ came into His kingdom. Jesus' reply demonstrated His matchless mercy, "Truly I say to you today, you shall be with Me in Paradise."

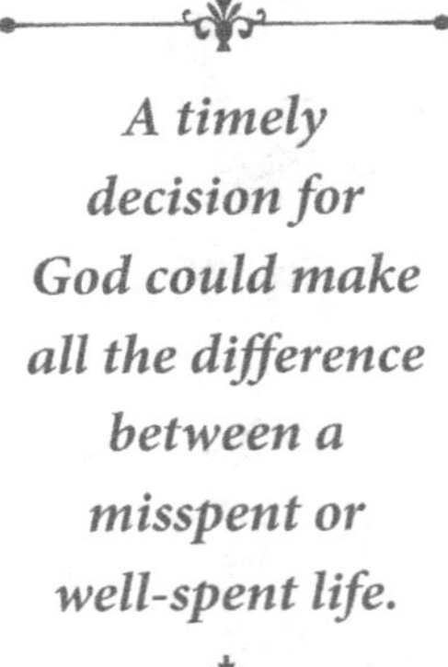

Although last-minute conversions are possible, and apparently probable, one would do well not to wait until the last minute to commit to God. A timely decision for God could make all the difference between a misspent or well-spent life. God's justice is often tempered with mercy, but the reverse is also true.

We cannot, therefore, assume that a loved one is not in heaven. We are not always privy to the decisions of others. As God clarifies in 2 Peter 3:9, He is "…not willing that any should perish, but that all should come to repentance." His generous promise, found in Romans 10:13, "For everyone who calls upon the name of the Lord shall be saved," is eternally irrevocable.

Particularly troubling is an all-too-common misunderstanding of the scriptural perspective concerning the death of a child or infant. If a loved one who was quite young has passed before reaching an age of accountability, scripture clearly indicates their automatic entrance into heaven. This concept flies in the face of prevailing religious doctrines including purgatory and the need for infant baptism.

A number of scriptures reflect Christ's lovely attitude toward children, but the definitive is found in Matthew 19:14: "But Jesus said, Permit little children, and forbid them not, to come unto me; *for of such is the kingdom of heaven.*" As to the existence of purgatory, scripture peremptorily debunks the myth of the existence of a stopover en route to a final destination. As 2 Corinthians 5:8 clearly states, "to be absent from the body is to be present with the Lord." There is no scriptural indication whatsoever that a child, or anyone of any age, will be kept in a holding pattern awaiting purification.

Therefore, scripturally speaking, there is no documented lag time, or any condition that needs to be met or fulfilled, that would bar a child upon their death from being immediately ushered into the presence of God. One should consider the millions of babies that have been either miscarried or aborted. A just God would never deny the entrance of the innocent, nor relegate a child to a requirement impossible to fulfill. We can rest assured that according to scriptural promises, a baby or young child who has passed is even now securely residing in the presence of God.

***

That fateful balloon ride was an enormously illustrative one. If this would indeed be the day of my death, I wondered whether I had prepared adequately. Had I lived well, served well? Was my mission over? Would I finally hear the words I so longed for, "Well done, good and faithful servant." (Matthew 25:23) It was a cleansing and starkly clarifying reverie.

As it happened, on that day, our lives were mercifully spared. Landing arrangements at last secured, our pilot—inexplicably unruffled—began the process of skillfully releasing hot air from the balloon, deftly guiding our gradual descent to earth. It was immensely gratifying to see the ground grow ever closer. Unable to navigate back to our launch site, we instead bumpily landed on the reservation, basket lurching sideways, to a waiting group of first responders, including police officers, EMT's, and Pueblo council members.

We later discovered that our pilot was none other than Troy Bradley, world-renowned balloonist, prolific record-setter in the sport, and unquestionably one of the country's most competent and experienced pilots. I couldn't have been in better hands.

My Father's of course!

"Ask where has the fire carried the forests it has devoured? Or where has the flood borne away the navies it has swallowed up? To call back these harvests would be a task which only madness could attempt. Fly, swift-winged angels, but you cannot overtake the spoilers—neither could your eyes of fire detect the caverns in which the robbers have stored their wealth. The fruits of wasted years are gone, gone past hope. Yet, behold, the Lord who called light out of darkness and will yet bring forth life from the tomb, declares that these long-lost spoils shall be restored! And shall it not be done? Is anything too hard for the Lord? ***Does not the very difficulty, yes, impossibility of the enterprise make it the more worthy of the Almighty?"***

—C.H. SPURGEON

"And I will restore to you the years that the locust has eaten."

—Joel 2:25

"For this corruptible must put on incorruption, and this mortal must put on immortality. So, when this corruptible shall have put on incorruption, and this mortal shall have put on immortality, then shall be brought to pass the saying that is written, Death is swallowed up in victory."

"O death, where is thy sting? O grave, where is thy victory?"

—1 Corinthians 15:53-55

NOTES

All Scripture quotations, unless otherwise indicated, are taken from The Holy Bible. King James Version. New York: Thomas Nelson, 1972.

Scripture quotations marked (NIV) are taken from the Holy Bible, New International Version®, NIV®. Copyright © 1973, 1978, 1984, 2011 by Biblica, Inc.™ Used by permission of Zondervan. All rights reserved worldwide. **www.zondervan.com** The "NIV" and "New International Version" are trademarks registered in the United States Patent and Trademark Office by Biblica, Inc.™

Scripture quotations marked (Weymouth) are taken from The Holy Bible. Weymouth, Richard Francis. *New Testament in Modern Speech.* Grand Rapids, MI: Kregel Publications, 1978.

Scripture quotations marked (NKJV) are taken from the New King James Version®. Copyright © 1982 by Thomas Nelson. Used by permission. All rights reserved.

Pg. 5

Lewis, C. S. *The Weight of Glory: And Other Essays*. New York: Macmillan, 1949.

Pg.19

Lewis, C. S. *A Grief Observed*. London: CrossReach Publications, 2016.

A Grief Observed by CS Lewis © copyright CS Ltd 1961.

Nee, Watchman. *The Collected Works of Watchman Nee*. Anaheim, CA: Living Stream Ministry, 1992.

Pg. 21 & 25

Lewis, C. S. *The Problem of Pain*. Glasgow: Collins, 1977.

The Problem of Pain by C. S. Lewis © copyright CS Lewis ©Pte Ltd 1940.

Pg. 31

Manning, Brennan. *The Ragamuffin Gospel*. CO Springs, CO: Multnomah Books, 2015.

Pg. 33

Tada, Joni Eareckson. *Heaven: Your Real Home*. Grand Rapids, MI: Zondervan, 2001. Used by permission.

Pg. 35

Tyndale, William. *The Obedience of a Christian Man*, 1528.

Pg. 37

Guyon, Jeanne Marie Bouvier De La Motte. *Madame Guyon: An Autobiographie (classique Reprint). (Kindle Locations 98-99).*

Kierkegaard, Soren Aabye. *Works of Love: First Series.* Harper, 1962.

Pg. 38

Miriamwebster.com

Pg. 44

Advertising piece for a Billy Graham crusade.

Pg. 60

MacDonald, George. *Unspoken Sermons: Series I, II, III in One Volume.* Memphis, TN: Bottom of the Hill Publishing, 2012.

Pg. 66

Chesterton, G. R. *What I Saw in America.* London, 1922.

Pg. 72

Marty, Martin E. *Dietrich Bonhoeffer's "Letters and Papers from Prison": A Biography.* Princeton University Press, 2011. http://www.jstor.org/stable/j.ctt7rmsf.

Pg. 75

Tozer, A.W. *Worship the Reason We Were Created—Collected Insights.* Chicago: Moody Publishers, 2017.

Pg. 81

Keller, Helen. Interview quote. June 26, 1955.

Elliot, Elizabeth. *Facing the Death of Someone You Love.* Illinois: Good News Publishers, 1982. Used by permission.

Pg. 82

Tolkien, J. R. R. *(1937),* Douglas A. Anderson, ed., *The Annotated Hobbit, Boston:* Houghton Mifflin (published 2002), *"Riddles in the Dark", ISBN 0-618-13470-0.*

Tolkien, J. R. *Return of the King 1955, Appendix A: I (iv), pp. 335–6.*

Pg. 85

Ghandi, Mahatma. Paraphrase of a Persian proverb: *The Gulistan of Sa'di,* 1258.

Pg. 90

Buechner, Frederick. *Godric.* San Francisco: Harper, *1990.*

Pg. 97

Muir, John, and Linnie M. Wolfe. *John of the Mountains the Unpubl. Journals of John Muir.* Temecula, CA: Repr. Services, 1991.

Pg. 104

Drummond, Henry. *Addresses.* Moody Publishers, 1990.

Pg. 108

Graham, Billy, Press conference in Poland. 1978. Used by permission.

Chambers, Oswald. *My Utmost for His Highest: The Classic Daily Devotional.* Uhrichsville, OH: Barbour Books, 2015.

Pg. 121

Bunyan, John. *The Pilgrim's Progress: In Two Parts.* Boston: Judson Press, 2019.

EXCERPT FROM THE AUTHOR'S COMPANION BOOK:

MISSING LISA: A PARENT GRIEVES

AUGUST 2001

I am trying the beach again. I am calmer now than in days past, my attitude no longer constructing an impenetrable wall between God and me. I know I can always choose whether or not to construct that wall. I think it safe to say that the problem of impaired communication almost inevitably lies at the foot of the receiving side.

Lately my soul has become saturated with the sound of my own rants. The unchecked torrents of words drown the still small voice of God's Spirit. They hinder my capacity to think clearly and to process. I wish I could keep them quiet.

It is a different feel today. The water is an azure calm, waves gently breaking in tiny ripples, unperturbed in the way I would love to be. The sky mirrors the ocean's depth and grandeur. Best of all, there is no one else in sight. I am now always immensely relieved to be alone.

The setting is majestic and warmly inviting, yet I feel terribly lost. I want God to locate me—to cut through this veil of pain and reveal His Grace. I ask to be given a sign, hoping that in doing so I will not be perfunctorily aligning myself with the evil and faithless generation mentioned in the New Testament. (Matthew 16:4)

I ask anyway. This time I want a better sign than the typical asymmetrical, lumpy, and almost indistinguishable as heart-shaped, stone or shell. Shapes that strain even my credulity. I ask to see a perfectly heart-shaped sign. (*"God, if you really love me…"*). I am testing Him, and I don't care.

Two steps further and I see something on the sand. This can't be. My eyes are surely playing tricks.

I reach down and pick it up—a large, brilliant yellow, perfectly symmetrical, molded *plastic* heart.

Very funny.

No, really. I am laughing.

Lynne Little Ministries is a 501(c)(3) organization whose mission is to utilize faith-based principles to affirm, strengthen and assist those who have experienced profound loss and to help those individuals discover purpose and find the courage to move forward. For additional resources, help, and encouragement visit: lynnelittle.org

Printed in the USA
CPSIA information can be obtained
at www.ICGtesting.com
JSHW081117250224
57931JS00001B/6